Live Long and Prosper

How to Understand, Build and Protect Your Perfect Pension

Paul Lewis

A & C Black • London

First published in Great Britain 2006

A & C Black Publishers Ltd
38 Soho Square, London W1D 3HB

British Library Cataloguing in Publication Data
A CIP record for this book is available from the British Library.

ISBN-10: 0–7136–7502–0
ISBN-13: 978–0–7136–7502–3

A & C Black uses paper produced with elemental chlorine-free pulp, harvested
from managed sustainable forests.

Design by Fiona Pike, Pike Design, Winchester
Typeset by RefineCatch Limited, Bungay, Suffolk
Printed in Great Britain by William Clowes Ltd, Beccles, Suffolk

5/06

CONTENTS

ACKNOWLEDGEMENTS

Many, many people have helped me with this book – financial advisers (independent of course), civil servants (anonymous naturally), actuaries (making sense of financial ramblings), researchers (many), press officers (loads), and thinkers (a few). Some of them, or the organisations they run or work for, are mentioned in the text. Others are in the contacts at the end. And even more are not mentioned at all. It's not the Oscars after all. But they know who they are. And they, above all, will know that any errors are mine, not theirs. Oh, and my mum. Who taught me so much. If only she'd brought everyone up.

ABOUT THE AUTHOR

Paul Lewis has been a prize-winning freelance finance journalist for 20 years. Currently he presents Money Box on BBC Radio 4 and writes extensively on personal finance and money in a wide variety of publications including *Saga Magazine*, the *Daily Telegraph* and *Reader's Digest*. He has written several books on managing money, tax and saving and writes for both Age Concern and Help the Aged on pensions, social security and tax.

Outside the world of money he is an authority on the Victorian writer Wilkie Collins and co-editor of the first complete edition of his letters, published in June 2005. He is now working on a definitive bibliography of Collins. Paul runs his own website at: **www.paullewis.co.uk**

CHAPTER ONE

Start Here

I was really excited writing this book. And I am really pleased you're reading it – because I know that if you follow at least some of the advice in it, you will be richer in retirement. In other words you will keep more of your own money. And the Chancellor, financial advisers and your employer will keep a bit less. Of course they'll all keep some of it, that is just the way the world works. But because saving for your retirement can take a lot of your hard-earned dosh, every penny you can save helps achieve that goal of a perfect pension.

Being richer in retirement is simple, but it's not easy. Just like slimming. If you eat less, you'll lose weight – or gain it more slowly. After all, that material that makes up your body has to come from somewhere and your mouth is the only candidate. But the multi-billion-pound industry in slimming books, plans, diets and surgery is a testament to how not easy this simple advice is.

It's the same with pensions. It actually is simple to have a good retirement. It just means you have to have a much less good working life – and that's not an exchange many people will make. So this book explains how much you should save (I promise it'll be without boring bits so trust me, even that will be interesting, if a bit frightening); how you can use and abuse the system to maximise the amounts you do save; what will happen if you don't save (there is some comfort here actually because it may not be that bad – though it won't be very good either) and shines a bit of light on all those tedious rules that still exist even after the whole system was radically simplified this year.

Sir Clement Freud, when he passed 80, used to say he was at the age when if a woman said 'come upstairs and make love with me', he could only reply, 'I can do either one but not both'. Today we might give the same answer to a passing Vulcan who greets us with the words, 'Live Long and Prosper'. I might do one, but not both. The salutation was first heard on the science fiction TV series *Star Trek* on 17 November 1967. Ah, the sixties. We did not know then how things would change – how much our lives would lengthen and our expectations of prosperity would grow.

This book won't help you live any longer. People are managing that without my help. But it will help you to prosper.

Enjoy.

WHY NOW?

There are two reasons to publish the book. First, April 2006 is the month of A-Day: not just A-for-any-old day, but of *the* A-Day itself. We'll come to what the 'A' stands for later, but A-Day is important – a bonfire of inanities when all sorts of stupid pension rules go up in smoke. Forget Guy Fawkes; April 6 2006 makes nearly a ton of gunpowder under the entire ruling class pale into insignificance. Fifty years of rules and restrictions, all of which were considered vital at one time or another, are being vaporised. From 6 April 2006 they all go for good – in both senses of the word.

And second – complexification. I didn't make that word up; you will find it in the very longest version of the Oxford English Dictionary. Since it first appeared 90 years ago, it has been taken up (mainly by scientists) to describe just what you'd expect – the way stuff has a habit of becoming more complex the longer it goes on. Like life.

The way I use it, complexification is definitely not benign, because it is not a natural process. It is a dark side word, the malign twin of 'simplification' which is generally good. Complexification works against understanding. For example, income tax is a really simple idea: the higher your income, the more is taken off it in tax. Anyone can understand that and see it is fair. Since its invention in England in 1798 – sadly but perhaps inevitably to fund a war – income tax has come to raise the bulk of government revenue throughout the world (only seven nations do not have any personal income tax: five of them are tax havens and two are small oil-rich states). But hard work by generations of accountants and politicians has made it almost impossible to understand. It has been complexified – and that keeps armies of people in work calculating it, raising it, checking it and avoiding it.

However, the complexification I really complain about (because I quite like accountants) is in the area of selling things. Companies complicate so that potential customers find it hard to make rational choices. As a result they make mistakes, pick the wrong product, pay too much, and the business profits from the mistakes. It is all so complex that customers seldom realise they have been duped – and if they do, it is impossible to prove.

Complexification is not normally applied to material stuff like cornflakes, but to what I call intangible things. Phone tariffs are one good example. They used to be simple: you picked up the phone, made a call and were charged for every minute until you put it down again. But now it is almost never possible to determine the cheapest way to make any particular call. Tariffs have been complexified. And in that confusion people lose money, while phone service providers make it. For 'phone' substitute gas, electricity, broadband and, of course, loads of financial products.

Pensions are bordering on the state of complexification, which is one reason why the subject needs whole books. (I hate to break it to you, other pension books are available. But you've started this one so you might as well finish.)

And despite the great shredding of red tape on A-Day, New Pensions, as we might call them, are already becoming complexified.

The intention was good. It went like this:

★ **People are not saving enough for their retirement.**
★ **One of the things that stops them is the complex set of rules that surround how, and how much, you can save in a pension.**
★ **Let's get rid of those complex rules.**

So on A-Day, just about all the rules that existed were swept away and replaced with . . . well, more rules. Because the problem is that pensions come with a huge public subsidy. Unlike anything else you buy, you do not have to pay tax on the money you spend on pensions. However, you have already paid tax on the money that's in your bank account – it's taken off your pay before you see it. So when you spend some of that money by investing in a pension, the taxman has to give back the tax you have already paid. Officially that rebate cost the country £12,300,000,000 (£12.3 billion) in 2004/05 and today the official cost is probably approaching £15 billion. If the Chancellor got rid of the rebate, he could slash the basic rate of income tax by 4p in the £. So even with the New Pensions there have to be rules to make sure that money is being put into pensions to provide for retirement, rather than just to get the tax relief. More than half of the tax subsidy goes to the richest eighth of the population (those who pay higher-rate tax). . . just the ones who might try to take a bit more. So a lot of the restrictions that have been introduced are about making sure that it's the pension, not the tax relief, which is the main point of any pension investment that gets this subsidy.

Anorak's note. The net cost of tax relief is a tricky set of sums. In 2004/05 the total tax rebates paid to people investing in pensions was around £17.8 billion. To that you have to add the £2.6 billion cost of charging no tax on the growth in the fund, another £214 million for National Insurance rebates to personal pensions and £300 million for tax-free lump sums from some schemes. From that total of £20.9 billion, the Treasury deducts the £8.6 billion income tax which is paid by people who already receive a pension. It argues that if saving up was not tax free, then the pensions paid out would be. So you end up with a net cost of £12.3 billion (according to HM Revenue & Customs, but £12.4 billion in the Treasury table. But hey, what's a spare £100 million when you are talking pensions?). At this point many commentators believe

> you should add on another £6.8 billion, which is ignored by the Treasury – that is the cost of not charging National Insurance on the pension contributions paid by employers. Adding that boosts the total cost to a shade over £19 billion in 2004/05. Or £27.6 billion if you do not buy the argument that pensions would be tax free if saving up for them wasn't. Not so much complexification as obfuscation – hiding the real cost of a massive subsidy going to the half of the population who have a pension (and mainly to the richest eighth of them) and being paid for equally by the other – generally poorer – half, who do not.

So although the new rules are simpler than the 50 years of legislation they replace, the Pensions Act 2004 (which brought in some of the rules) and the Finance Act 2004 (which brought in most of the rest) and the Regulations (which deal with the fiddly bits) and the guidance manuals (which explain how you should interpret what you read in the Acts and Regulations) already amount to thousands of pages.

So although A-Day was a major simplification, all those people whose job it has been for two generations to complexify stuff – I mean accountants, politicians, Treasury officials, tax inspectors and, not least, the lawyers – have already been busy making sure they will stay in work at least until they can draw their own pensions.

This book does not contain all the detail (but I hope it contains most of what you need) and it is possible that some things have changed since I wrote it. Actually that's inevitable, which is why there is a website which will contain updates and tables and spreadsheets and links and fun stuff like that. See how sad I am – I find spreadsheets fun. But put it this way: on a cold and windy day with rain already spitting down, wouldn't you rather be with your anorak than without? In the stormy world of pensions, I am that anorak.

JARGON

Before we go much further, let me say now I don't like TLAs. I believe they are a BTU and a JHP. Bad enough that people have DNIs in a book like this without hiding them in YAT.

See glossary below.

> **BTU** – Barrier To Understanding
> **DNI** – Difficult New Ideas
> **JHP** – Jargon Hiding Place
> **TLA** – Three Letter Abbreviation
> **YAT** – Yet Another TLA

Still a bit tricky isn't it? How much simpler if I had written it in English:

Let me say now I don't like acronyms, usually in the form of three-letter abbreviations. I believe they get in the way of understanding things and can be used as a hiding place for jargon. And jargon is bad enough when it is out in the open without giving it a cloak of abbreviation to lurk under. There are enough strange new ideas in a book like this without hiding them in yet another TLA. Whoops!

Well, you see what I mean. So I will refrain from using TLAs and AOSOYs (Any Other Sort Of Abbreviations) generally, apart from a few exceptions – things that are common currency. But I won't assume that because I have explained that FSA means the Financial Services Authority on p. 6, you will remember that when you are struggling with p. 178. So although there will be a few abbreviations I will mainly use real words, or what pass for real words in the weird world of pensions.

One way to tackle the growing use of abbreviations is to make up other things they could stand for. So FSA, which is the acronym of Financial Services Authority, could be – well you think of it. The rule of backronyms, as these are called, is that none of the words must be the same as original. So for example you couldn't have Flipping Stupid Authority because it still uses the word 'authority'. But you could have Fanny Sweet Adams, which is my favourite even though it is not true. The FSA actually does a lot and most of it is very useful at best and harmless at worst. We'll be coming across the FSA many times in this book, which is why I do abbreviate it from time to time. It saves ink and paper.

I also eschew exigent, otiose or recondite words. Like those. Some of the ideas of pensions are tricky, but there is nothing that cannot be explained in plain English and short, simple, everyday words. Well, except 'actuary', and I will explain that later. And somewhere in this book those four words will be used. The first person to email me the page numbers will get a reply. Sorry if that seems a mean reward, but I have to save my pennies for my pension fund.

WHY MUST WE SAVE FOR A PENSION?

A pension is the money we live on during the longest holiday of our lives – the years of our retirement. It might not be 20 years; it could be less, but it will probably be more. As we slog into work each day, we each hope that for us it will be at least that long. After a lifetime's work we surely deserve some time to enjoy ourselves at the end, don't we? A sort of gap year. Or more like a gap decade. Or two. Well, maybe. But the way things are going, this final holiday will be a long one and someone has to pay for it – after all we won't be working. And there aren't many candidates for sugar daddy. Let's think who they might be.

Other taxpayers, usually called 'the state'. The place we used to work – that's a company or employer's pension. Ourselves through our own savings, either a pension or maybe a string of houses. A rich relative who dies at the right moment and leaves us loads of money. A spouse – but return to Go because they have to get the money from somewhere too. Erm, I'm running out of ideas here. I know, the lottery. After all we have a 14-million-to-one chance of winning and every week someone gets lucky. Ditto premium bonds: two million-aires every month they make, though the odds on a single bond winning are 14 billion to one. Someone you meet in a bar who gives you a load of cash and doesn't expect sex in return (or perhaps they do, but hey – it's a pension!).

As you can see, I have run out of ideas. And realistically, as far as planning rather than hoping is concerned, only the first three count.

Now I am going to disappoint you. They are all the same – the state, your employer and you. Whoever provides your pension, the money actually comes from the same people: those who are working when you have retired. Now this is a bit of a subtle one, but stick with me.

It is easy to see who pays if the state provides your pension. It happens in many European countries: everyone gets a pension at 65, related to what they have earned in work. For example, in France people typically get a state pension which is half their average pay in their best 25 years in work. Even in the good old 'we're-so-self-reliant-we-don't-need-welfare' USA, the state pays everyone who has worked a generous old-age pension (usually called social security) of roughly 30% of their pay up to a maximum of around £13,000 a year. And who pays? Yes, other people who are still taxpayers. Our own state pension works this way too. Look at your pay slip. That item labelled NI or National Insurance contributions is a tax that is used mainly to pay the pensions of people currently retired.

So the state is easy. Today's workers pay for today's pensioners – just as today's pensioners paid for the pensioners when they themselves were at work. It's a bargain between the generations. The trouble is that today's workers pay the pensions of older folk, but cannot possibly know if younger folk will be willing to do that for them in future.

That's why it is important to – pause for trumpets – Save For Our Own Future. It's the Thatcher dream all over again. Because in the 1980s, that was the Big Idea: don't rely on the state; save for your own future.

Now that Big Idea has two problems. First, the more you save now, the less you have to spend and the less trade there is and the less the economy grows and the fewer people have jobs and . . . well you get the picture. Second, however much you save, you have to live off

that when you stop working. In order for your savings to be converted into an income, they have to carry on earning money and
grow, and that means dividends on shares or interest on savings, and
that means that companies are doing well, and that means people are
in work and using their money to buy stuff (and save for their own
pension). Alternatively of course you can save up so much that it just
sits there and you spend it slowly over the rest of your life. But for
that to work, inflation has to be low so it retains its value and that
depends on the economy being strong and growing and people being
in work and paying taxes and buying stuff and . . . have I made the
point yet?

Ultimately the value of the money you spend when you don't work
comes, one way or another, from the people who are in work when
you are not. And today's big idea is that there are going to be fewer of
them in the future – or at least fewer of them for each person who has
stopped work. It goes by the name 'dependency ratio', and it means
the number of people in work to keep each of those who are not.

Not all those who do not work are retired. About a quarter of
working-age people do not earn money. Most of them still work of
course – bringing up children, caring for dependent relatives, or looking for a job. And then there are all those in school, college and university. They all have to be kept too.

Anyway, the ratio is going to get worse. The figures were set out by
Adair Turner in the Pensions Commission's first report in October
2004. He told me then that he wanted his first report to provide 'a
real, clear and undebateable set out of the facts'.

According to Turner, in 1960 the dependency ratio was around five to
one. In other words there were five people in work for each one who
was not, young and old. (In fact the ratio compares the number of
people aged 20–64 with the total number under 20 and over 65. So it
is a bit rough and ready, but Turner decided it would do.) Today it is
around three and a half to one, where it has been for some time. But it
is about to nosedive, heading to 3:1 by 2015 and to almost 2:1 by 2040.

So in 35 years, each non-working person will be kept by only two other people.

Now if I am right that the income of non-workers depends on those who do work, then there is a problem here. Whatever we do, we will end up poorer in retirement. Or almost whatever we do.

In his first report in 2004 Adair Turner said that there were only four choices for the future. We could work longer, save more, pay more tax, or be poorer. In truth if the dependency ratio is going to change as he predicted, then neither saving more nor paying more tax works. Being poorer of course may well happen. But working longer is the only option that would change the dependency ratio. It would cut down the number of people over 65 who were dependent. That is why I think it is the only solution to the pensions crisis.

Pause here for a thought. There are two possible pension crises. First, there is the one that might strike **society as a whole**. That is the one that Adair and the politicians worry about – they worry about everyone. Second, there is the one that might strike **you**. And as with so many things, the way to solve your problem is different from the way to solve everyone's. Indeed, it may simply not be possible for everyone to be rich in retirement – any more than everyone is rich at 30 or 40. This book is really about you, not society as a whole. Leave that to clever folk like Adair.

Meanwhile, you can try to protect yourself by saving as much as you can while you are working. But however much you save will be of no use to you if the younger generations are not working and spending while you sip a gin and tonic on the terrace. In fact if they are not working and spending, you will not be sipping a gin and tonic on the terrace because gin will be £1,283 a bottle, and tonic – well, that quinine will put the price up to around £84 a mixer.

There is an alternative to Adair's gloomy view of the dependency ratio, because whenever you get three economists in a lift you get four opinions about which way it is going. Find out more in What crisis? on p. 40.

HOW MUCH SHOULD I SAVE?

There is an answer to this question and we will come to it before the end of this chapter, honest. But first you have to ask yourself what you want in retirement. You can of course save nothing. If you do that then you will be relying on the state. Broadly speaking, the state expects you to live on £114.05 a week. If your income is less than that, then the state will make it up to that level. Now £114.05 a week is £5,931 a year and is about as much as the typical person in work earns in just over a day. So what you now earn in a week will have to last you about a month.

Actually it is not quite as bad as that, because a person in work pays tax and National Insurance whereas someone over pension age pays no National Insurance (even if they work) and, at 65, no tax is due on an income this low. So this £5,931 should be compared with your earnings after tax and National Insurance has been taken off – your 'take-home' pay. The guaranteed state pension of £114.05 a week works out to around a third of the take-home pay of someone on typical earnings. So if you save nothing and your earnings are pretty bog-standard, then by relying on the state you will be living on around a third of your net income in work. For every £60 you take out of the cash machine now, you will have just £20. Could you live on that? I couldn't.

You'll notice I did a bit of arithmetic in the last paragraph. It was £114.05 × 52 = £5,931. There are quite a few sums in this book. It is all very simple stuff – like £20 is a third of £60 and I explain it as clearly as I can. But I know some people do find numbers difficult. It often helps to use a calculator either to check what I write – 'Oh yes. It does come to that! Who'd have thought it?' – or to put in your own details and see what the arithmetic tells you. If you don't have a calculator, buy one! If you do, you'll see that £114.05 × 52 = £5930.60 which I rounded up to £5931. There will be quite a bit of rounding too, usually silent rounding. But if things don't quite add up or work out, it is rounding that is to blame.

I am old enough to remember the time before there were calculators. My Dad gave up teaching to sell them when they first came out. You set the dials and then did the sums by turning a handle on these mechanical miracles. Of course sometimes they would jam, normally at the end of a long calculation just before you got the answer. Back to pencil and paper. Around 1970 I was amazed to see my first electronic calculator, one of the first in the UK – a Sharp Compet. The size of a typewriter, it cost about £400 which is equivalent to more than £4,000 today, and could only add, subtract, multiply and divide (except by zero which sent it haywire). Today you can get a thumb-sized machine which will do all the arithmetical things you could ever need in a normal life, including sending a missile to the moon, for about £4.95. So buy one. It is never too late to get a bit more numerate.

Before we look at what you have to save in order to do better than the state will offer you, a word of warning. The state pension is not that simple. In fact a recent report commissioned by the Government criticised its 'bewildering complexity'. We will examine it in detail in Chapter 4 'State Supremacy? Will the State provide?' and we will see that for some people in some circumstances, the answer to that question is actually a resounding 'yes'. But we are going to ignore those complexities here. First, because the state pension really does need a chapter (or a book!) to itself and second, because it may be radically reformed in the next few years and be entirely different by the time you retire. So relying on the present state pension in the future has its dangers, whereas the arithmetic of what you have to save will stay the same. As maths does.

The first question is, what will a decent income be in retirement? We don't know how much pay will be then, or prices. What will a loaf of bread cost? Or a car? Or running a house? And what will we spend then that we don't spend now? Who would have thought of Sky or laptops or broadband or mobile phones 40 years ago?

Wages always rise faster than the price of things we buy. That is how the economy works. So if our pension is as good as a decent wage, then we will be able to manage. Now, what a decent wage is partly depends on what we currently earn. So the easiest way to say what we will need in retirement is to ask what income is a fair proportion of what we earn now. It would be a bit greedy to expect to have the same income. When you retire, you will pay less tax and save all those expenses related to work – so the same income would leave you better off for doing no work. Dream on! As you will not need quite as much money, a decent income in retirement is normally assumed to be around half or two thirds of what you earn in work. Without all those expenses, two thirds will leave you not much worse off and a half should still be OK. But much less will leave you in difficulties – few can live easily on an income which is a third or a quarter of what they are used to in work. So whatever you earn, your aim is to achieve a pension of at least half or, if you're more ambitious, two thirds of that when you retire.

At this point you may be wondering how much are average earnings – and how you compare. Well, it is a simple question but it takes several volumes of complex tables to answer it to the satisfaction of Government statisticians. That is partly because number crunchers make their living out of making things complicated – or, as they would say, 'being thorough and getting things right'. (Note that this is different from complexification, which is a deliberate process of making things hard to understand in order to trick people out of money.) But it's also partly because there are lots of things we might mean by 'what does the average person earn?'. Average pay depends on your age (it peaks between 30 and 50) and your sex (despite 30 years of laws against sex discrimination, men still earn about a quarter more than women. If average female pay were £400 a week, then average male pay would be £500. So it's probably best to keep men and women separate – don't worry, you can get together again later). But then there is basic pay, overtime pay, reductions for sickness (not everyone gets paid in full when they are off ill), part-time work (mainly women), regional differences and so on. Let's leave all those to the statisticians for a bit and find what we all want – one figure for men and one for women of any age over the whole UK, in full-time work and who are not being penalised for being sick.

> **WOMEN**
> The fact that women are paid less than men is only half the problem they face. Out of just over 12 million women in work, only 7 million of them work full time, the rest work part time. So even if they are paid the same rate for the job as men (and their jobs are as well paid as men's), they would earn less because they work fewer hours. Sorry, I'll rephrase that. They do less paid employment because – as we all know – it often falls to them to look after children, other relatives and sometimes even (God forbid) their husband or boyfriend. Swap him for a decent job and a pension is my advice.

One final fiddly bit. There are two sorts of average. With one, you add up all the wages earned in the whole UK and divide them by the number of people who earn them. That is what we normally call the average – technically it's called the 'mean'. Or you can find the level of pay where half the population will earn less and half the population will earn more. That is called the 'median' and is the best one to use for 'average' pay. It is now used for all official figures because if you stick a pin in the population of the UK, the chances are that the person who yelps will earn this much. It's the half-way point.

So here are the figures, men and women separately and, as I promised, together.

Full time pay in UK 2005	Men	Women	Both together
Median (halfway point)	£25,112	£19,447	£22,941
Source: National Statistics. Annual Survey of Hours and Earnings 2005			

Now you're interested aren't you?

All of you: 'Gosh, is average pay around £23,000?'

One half of you: 'I knew my pay was poor but I didn't realise I was in the bottom half of earnings, and well in it by the looks.'

The other half: 'I don't believe my pay is above average. I can hardly manage on it. Is that really what average pay is? How does anyone afford a house?!'

Person with a pin sticking out of them: 'Gosh, my pay is exactly typical. Ouch!'

Now you're wondering how far you are from the average, aren't you? Are you in the top quarter? So at a party with 40 people, will you be one of the top ten earners? Or maybe you are in the bottom tenth – so that for every ten people you pass on the street, only one will be as badly paid as you? Here are the figures.

Full-time pay UK 2005	Men	Women	Both together
Top tenth	£50,116	£36,618	£44,906
Top quarter	£35,012	£28,000	£32,200
Median (halfway point)	£25,112	£19,447	£22,941
Bottom quarter	£18,086	£14,133	£16,271
Bottom tenth	£13,744	£10,887	£12,270
Source: National Statistics, Annual Survey of Hours and Earnings, 2005.			

So if your pay is £36,000, you are in the top quarter but below the top tenth. If it is £10,000 you are in the bottom tenth. Now don't feel too bad – or indeed too smug. It may be related to where you live. I know I said we would ignore regional differences, but the truth is that pay is very much more in London (half-way point £29,903) than anywhere else – even in the rest of south east England it is a lot less at £24,286. The lowest in the UK is Northern Ireland (£20,148) and it is slightly more (£20,366) in north east England.

So now you know how your pay compares. And we have decided that whatever you are paid (and don't be too depressed, you might get a better job next month), the target for a pension should be half to two thirds of that. So what do you have to save to achieve that income in retirement? Working it out can seem very difficult. It is impossible to predict the future, but there are three things we need to know. How much will you be earning in 30 years' time? How much will your savings grow each year? How long will you live? The truth is no-one knows the answer to any of those questions. However, there is a group of professionals who make it their job to work them out. They are called actuaries and they use what they call 'assumptions' about all these things (also known as 'wild guesses').

The word 'actuary' comes from the Latin for 'clerk', rather than prophet; the Romans had a healthy disdain for their prophets, who were commonly mocked in plays. Indeed, the words for 'guess' such as 'divino' and 'auguror' also had meanings related to prophecy. Professor Peter Jones is a classical scholar who suggested to me that 'amenaugur' – mad guesser – is the closest we can get to what an actuary might have been called if such a job had existed in the Roman world. But mad guesser is a bit mean to the actuarial profession. Actuaries say themselves that they 'make financial sense of the future' (honest, it's on their website). In a sense they do what statisticians do about the past. So just as the latter are number crunchers, actuaries might be called future crunchers.

Back to these guesses – sorry, assumptions. They are generally based on the simple belief that what has happened in the past will carry on happening in the future. It's the same principle that keeps turkeys happy as the end of December approaches.

'Gobble, gobble. Oh good, it's morning. Here comes the farmer with the food. Gobble, gobble. What is he holding? Gobble, gobble. A new kind of food, long and sharp, gobble, gob . . . '

You might spot the Christmas turkey principle in other chapters. But when you are working out what you have to put aside for your retirement, wild guesses are not really what you want (in a minute, a technique for controlling them).

First, a reminder of our target – half to two thirds of what you are earning when you retire, that's the aim. Remember though that when NASA sent the Mars Climate Orbiter to the red planet in December 1998, mission controllers aimed for it to land on the surface, gently. But the $125-million spacecraft missed the target. It turned out that the engineers at NASA were working in feet and pounds while the onboard computer worked in metres and kilograms – so no surprise it missed. Even with hundreds of engineers, mathematicians and scientists involved, a small vehicle can miss a very big target. Thank God there were no actuaries at NASA. The orbiter might have turned round and crashed on London!

Anyway, we must get down to earth too and look at these pesky assumptions. The target is a proportion of wages, so we need to know how much they will grow over the next 20 or 40 years. And the vehicle heading for that target is our savings. How much will they grow over the same period? We don't really know. But looking at history, we do know that they grow at pretty much the same rate.

At the moment earnings grow by around 4.5% a year. And, by a happy coincidence, the long-term rate of growth of investments after you've paid the charges for someone to look after them is also around 4.5% a year. So, as we used to say in my school maths class, they 'cancel out'. Or rather we used to say, 'Sir, do they cancel out?' And Mr Blake would look over his rimless glasses and say prissily, 'No they do not 'cancel out'. That is an operation we do not recognise in mathematics. But if you divide both sides by the same number, then they each become one – and so effectively disappear.' So there. But this isn't a maths lesson, so we'll just say they cancel out. Looking at it this way, we can see that the investment growth simply keeps our savings up with the overall rise in wages. So forget all the talk about what money is 'worth' now and how much it will be 'in real terms' in the future. Let investment growth take care of that and use today's pounds to work it out. That way we will avoid the Mars Orbiter problem; we'll use the same units now and in the future.

You might say this is all a bit simplistic. I can see wise financial services industry heads referring me to projections (another word for wild guesses) by the Financial Services Authority suggesting that investments will grow by 7% a year. Or to the Government Actuary himself, Future Cruncher in Chief, Chris Daykin, who assumes that investment growth will be 2% a year ahead of earnings growth. And there will be those who remember fondly that heady time in the last quarter of the 20th century when investments in shares grew by 12% a year every year – forgetting that over the next three and a bit years they plummeted to less than half their value and have still not recovered (though to be fair they have been growing at quite a rate for the last three years).

I remind them that this is not just the bright idea of a two-bit financial journalist (me). It was put forward to me by one of Britain's top actuaries. His name is Tom Ross, past President of the Faculty of Actuaries, and a man who has been around the pension industry so long he has already started to draw one of his several pensions. As Tom himself might put it: if you are going to make wild guesses, why not make one that simplifies the arithmetic?

So we come to my calculator. I call it the Ross Ice Sheet – first, because it is based on that idea first given to me by Tom Ross; second, it is a spreadsheet. And third, when people see it they get an icy shiver down their spine which makes −40°C in the Antarctic seem positively warm. Because it says you have to save a third of your pay from the age of 20 to have a pension when you retire equal to half the income you enjoyed in work.

'I have to save HOW much?'

OK. That is a normal reaction.

'That's it. This mad book told me I had to save a third of my income to have a decent pension. So I stopped reading it.'

Normal again.

'I mean either it's bollocks, and I should bin it or give it to Oxfam

or something. Or it's true and I'll just give up. No way can I do that.'

That's normal too.

But it isn't bollocks, as you daintily call it. It is the truth. That is the problem with arithmetic: you can have an opinion or a guess, or make an estimate, but arithmetic tells you the truth. So you shouldn't throw this book away. Because we will now go on to discover how arithmetic can not only show the problem – it can also show us the way out.

When Tom Ross first showed me the calculation (actually he did it in his head over the phone, because whatever you say about actuaries they can do maths), he assumed we would work for 30 years and then have 30 years' retirement – because that is what many people still dream of. In modern terms of education and life expectancy, that means start work and saving at 20, stop at 50 and die at 80. Now no-one is really going to do that. Sorry to disappoint you but it's true (and why it's true is in Chapter 3 'Live Long and . . . Prosper?'). Suppose we admit that Tom's scenario is hopelessly over-optimistic. Suppose we start working and saving at 20 but, instead of stopping at 50, we wait until 60. That is 40 years' work and just 20 years' retirement. In that case, the proportion we need to save is just a fifth of our income. If we stop at 65 then it is a seventh – about 14 per cent – of what we earn. Now we are getting down to a possible amount. And remember that if you have a decent employer, then two thirds of that amount will be paid by them. The Ross Ice Sheet shows that if you pay 5% and your employer stumps up 10%, you can retire on half pay at around 64 and have 16 years to enjoy your retirement. So you see, the arithmetic is not there just to frighten you – it's also to show you what is needed.

Of course that calculation begs one question – did you start working and saving for a pension at 20? Because the age you put into the calculation is **not** the one where you start **work**. It is the age when you start **saving**. So if you are already 35 and you have not done any saving towards your pension yet, then it is '35' you put in, not your age on the magic day you first started earning a living. And just to put one more set of figures in it, suppose you are 35 and you do hope to retire at 60 and you do live until you are 80, then you will have to save about 2/7ths of your pay from now till you retire. In other words, for every £700 of monthly income, you need to put aside £200. If you earn £30,000 then you will have to put just over £8,500 a year into your pension – £714 a month. Icy chill down your spine yet?

You can play with the figures and put in what you think might happen to you by downloading the Ross Ice Sheet at **www.acblack.com/livelongandprosper**.

WOMEN

These figures make one assumption you will already have noticed (because girls do notice that sort of thing). They assume that you start work at one age and finish at retirement and do not stop in the middle to have babies. Now I know that can be a short interruption and good employers will pay you for the time you take off and Dads can also have paternity leave and we all live in a wonderful age of equality. But history shows that women have more gaps in their working lives than men do. And what do gaps mean? Smaller pensions. You can take account of them in the Ross Ice Sheet by assuming you start later. So if you started paying into a pension at 25 and you expect to have ten years off for kids, then assume you started at 35. It's rough and ready but hey, so is the whole thing.

So, that is the Ross Calculation or – as we might more grandly call it – the Ross-Lewis Approximation. How accurate is it? We don't know. We won't know until you reach 80, by which time Tom Ross and I will be safely protected from complaints by a local vicar who will blow the dust off an ancient computer and refer you to the plots where we are buried. And in fact you probably won't bother to complain, because 80 is the moment you will conveniently die as the money runs out. But cleverer and more meticulous people than

I (though not than Tom) have also done this calculation using much more complex assumptions and come up with similar answers.

For example, in January 2004 the Economic Affairs Committee of the House of Lords published a long report on what it called the 'economic aspects of an ageing population'. It got some calculations done on how much men and women of different ages had to save to achieve a pension of two thirds of their pay on retirement. These showed that a man who started saving for his pension at 35 needed to save 24% of his pay each year until he was 65 to have a reasonable chance of a pension worth two thirds of his salary. A woman needs to save more – 27%. That is because women live longer and need a bigger fund to provide their pension for more years. The Ross Ice Sheet ignores those effects. Even though slightly different assumptions were made, the table below is very similar to the figures given by the Ross Ice Sheet.

Required contributions to give a pension of two thirds final pay				
Starting age	25	35	45	55
	Percentage of salary required			
Men	17%	24%	37%	72%
Women	19%	27%	42%	84%
Assumptions: (1) earnings will rise 2% a year above inflation; (2) investments will grow at 3% a year above inflation				
Source: *Aspects of the Economics of an Ageing Population*, Select Committee on Economic Affairs, House of Lords Paper 179-1, January 2004 p. 42.				

It's comforting to know that my approximations agree with these detailed calculations – certainly for people under 45. It doesn't matter that the two tables disagree on some points. They both make assumptions and those may turn out to be wrong, but they both tell the same tale: in order to have a comfortable retirement, you have to save a lot of money. Probably more than you think you can.

> **Rule of Prosperity**
>
> **Save as much as you can into a good pension scheme and start as young as you can.**

But it is not hopeless. In fact we can all do enough. First, some people do not have to save a lot of money (later I explain who they are and why they are so lucky and advise them to make sure they stay that lucky). Second, as you work through the book you will be able to see how you can save and what that money will earn – and honestly it won't be as bad as you fear. Third, however much it turns out you have to save, this book will explain how to do it as safely, cheaply and effectively as possible—and save money elsewhere to help you do it. But don't take too long to read it. Because the sooner you start, the cheaper it will be to sort out A Perfect Pension.

Hang on. Something's been missed. What about the state pension? At the start of this bit, we said it could be a third of your take home pay all by itself. So if you save up enough to give a pension of half your income, then you will have a half plus a third, which is five sixths of your pay. And if you save up enough to get a pension of two thirds of pay, you will actually get 100% when the state pension is added in. So, you may ask, couldn't I just save enough to give me half or two thirds of my income **including** the state pension? That would be an easier target?

It's a fair question. In fact you haven't really been concentrating if that question wasn't in your mind at this point.

Here is my answer. First, the state pension is only a third if your earnings are at the mid point (around £22,000). If you earn much more than that, the state pension – which is a fixed amount of money – is less. Second, the state pension I described is means tested and if you have extra on top it will be less. That's what means testing is – a fine for thrift. Third, we know how the pension works now (well, sort of), but we do not know how it will work when you retire in 20, 30 or even 40 years from now. Fourth, the estimates of how much to save are approximations – OK, OK, they're wild guesses – so they may be wrong. The state pension performs the very useful function of filling that margin of error.

So ignore the state pension and save up as if it didn't exist. It may not when you retire. But, saying that, I don't want to take anything away from the state pension (whoops, I fell into football vernacular then) because the boy done good. You won't be, like, sick as a parrot, but you are not going to be over the moon my sunshine either. I do believe that for some people with below-average earnings, the state pension will be enough. See Chapter 4.

Right. Now we've sorted how much you should save. If you're impatient and want to see how much you are allowed to save you could skip to Chapter 7. But the short answer is 'as much as you want, just about, in most circumstances, or at least as much as you can afford.' So unless you really need all the detail now (yawn) just carry on with Chapter 2. Which is far more interesting. But Chapter 7 is far more useful if you want to know the detail.

CHAPTER TWO

Myths and Legends

Now, faced with **THE TRUTH** of how much you need to save and the knowledge that the new rules will not stop you saving that much, a natural reaction is to cast around looking for reasons why you shouldn't save for a pension now. And you don't have to look far. Excuses for not saving are as common as – well, the 12 million people who are not saving for their retirement. In this chapter I am going to look at all these excuses and demolish them one by one.

THEY'RE ALL CROOKS!

I am going to start with the tough one – for the financial services industry anyway. And whoever is shouting, 'I know – they're a bunch of crooks!' please desist. It is not true. There is a much more subtle explanation for the long succession of financial scandals where people have lost billions as the products they bought have failed to live up to the promises made by the people who sold them.

No lawful industry has been rocked by such a succession of scandals as financial services. In date order:

★ Mortgage endowments sold from the 1980s right up to the late 1990s will leave three million people up to £40 billion short of the money they need to repay their mortgages. Only £1 billion of compensation has been paid.
★ Personal pensions mis-sold to nearly two million people from 1988 to 1994 cost the industry £11.5 billion in compensation and another £2 billion in running the compensation scheme.
★ Between 1988 and 1994 at least 100,000 customers were sold the

wrong sort of Additional Voluntary Contributions (AVCs) to top up their company pensions. More than £250 million in compensation has been paid.

★ Split capital investment trusts were sold as safe investments, mainly from 1998 to 2002. Up to 50,000 individuals have lost at least £600 million. Compensation of £350 million was sought by the regulator. The industry finally coughed up £144 million – on condition that it admitted nothing and got indemnity from further action.

★ Precipice bonds were sold between 1997 and 2004 to 450,000 mainly older customers who wanted safety and a good return. They put in £7.4 billion and may have lost more than £2 billion.

Those are the big five – the devastating hurricanes that swept through the savings of ordinary honest folk and left them in ruins. There were other minor ones too, tropical storms which did less damage but still cost millions more folk millions more pounds as with-profits investments failed to produce any profits at all, pension unlocking was a waste of money, unnecessary insurance was sold, money put into shares failed to perform, and people were persuaded to invest in champagne or gold coins.

In the last four years, the Financial Services Authority has fined 76 companies and individuals more than £50 million and forced them to pay hundreds of millions of pounds in compensation for a variety of activities ranging from the misleading to the illegal. And forget icebergs – that is far less than 10% of what has really gone on under the water.

And like tropical storms, as one hits another is forming over the ocean, waiting to hit land and wreak more havoc. Mis-selling to people who were persuaded to opt out of SERPS is one brewing tempest (see p. 71 for more on that). Another is Venture Capital Trusts, where the main reason to invest was tax relief rather than a sound investment. And SIPPs (don't worry, I explain those in Chapter 6) were a thundercloud gathering before our very eyes until Flash Gordon (Brown—still hoping to Conquer the Universe) strode in and sorted it out in December 2005.

The mystery is not that the industry has lost the trust of its customers; the mystery is why anyone buys anything from it at all, ever.

I have almost talked myself into saying, 'OK you're right, it's all a waste of time. Throw this book away; better still, take it back to the bookshop claiming it was not fit for purpose under the Sale of Goods Act and buy a Jackie Collins novel instead'. But only almost. Because despite the succession of scandals – and notice how many times pensions are in there – saving for your future is very, very important. What do you earn now? How much do you spend? (And you can answer 'all of it', even though the truth is slightly more than that.) Can you live on what you earn? Could you live on half of it? You might have to. Half your salary is what most pensions that promise anything promise. Divide it by four, five, six, ten. Could you live on that? No? That is what this book protects you against. It is the airbag and seat belt on a journey through the financial jungle – and it is about more than mixed metaphors.

So, yes, there have been financial scandals. People have lost loads of money and even more have found that they have made far less than they hoped. But we do tend to hear about the bad news. The good news is that millions more have a better financial future, more security and, above all, more money than if they had not put some of their faith in the financial services industry. And the better equipped you are with knowledge, the better pension you will end up with.

MY HOME IS MY PENSION

I hear this a lot. My house is my pension. I have never understood it. It is the same as saying I don't need to buy a bed, I've got a sofa. Actually, it's more like saying I don't need a car, I've got castors on my sofa. A house is not a pension – and converting it into one is not going to be easy. If you have got three houses as well as the one you live in and they are all let out and when you retire you will be happy to live on the rent or sell the houses to give you a big lump-sum and live off that, then yes – those houses are your pension and good luck to you. You are sorted. As long as house prices stay up and the rental market stays strong, at any rate. It's just that most people are not in that position. But the house you live in is not a pension, and almost certainly will not provide one. Unless you live in a very large house that you inherited some time ago and it is worth a seven figure sum and you would be happy living somewhere else much cheaper – worth a small six figure sum – when you retire. Then maybe your house is your pension. These are exceptions. Generally, houses are not pensions.

Time for some arithmetic.

The average house in the UK (I use 'house' to mean anything which is a dwelling, flat, bungalow, semi, terraced or castle) is worth around £165,000 – or at least the ones that were sold last year were fetching that sort of price, on average. Suppose you have a house worth much more than that – let's say £250,000. A quarter of a million quid sounds like a lot; surely you can use that to provide a pension?

Well, you have to live somewhere and the most efficient way to get money out of your house is to sell it and buy somewhere cheaper – what they call 'trading down'. You might find a smaller place for half that, say £125,000. Leaving you with £125,000.

No. Life does not work like that. Every step of selling one house and buying another will cost you money (and hair, most likely, as you tear it out). First, a bit of a makeover. If you want to sell your home it will need tidying up, maybe a bit of painting, gardening, cleaning. Most of that you can do yourself, but reckon on £500 minimum for skip hire, paint, even a bit of lino to cover that stain. Then the estate agent. They act for you as seller, and they will charge between 1% and 2% of the price you get. In London where prices are much higher and the work is exactly the same, they charge even more than that. Let me run that past you again. In London where prices are higher and 2% of the price brings in more money than it does in say, Leicester, for the same work, they charge a **higher** percentage. And of course VAT is added to that. So negotiate and check it is comprehensive (you do not want another bill for the photographs or that video they play in their shop window). But you can still reckon the estate agent fees will be the biggest cost of moving.

Next you find somewhere you want. You need a survey. I know, you will not need a mortgage so no-one will make you have a survey – but come on, it is a house. You do not want to find the electrics are knackered, that a damp patch has been covered up with waterproof paint, that the under floor has dry rot, or even that suspicious new bit of lino is nailed over a nasty stain. Get a survey and reckon on £500. Or if you are doing this after some time in 2007, you might decide to rely on the compulsory Home Information Pack provided by the seller. Or you might not. And if it is after they become compulsory some time in 2007, add £1,000 onto your selling costs to pay for the Home Information Pack on the home you're selling.

Now you are going to need a solicitor, to do the paperwork for selling and buying. Reckon on £1,500 total to m'learned friends.

Then removal. Now, you might hire a van and dragoon three friends to move. But when you retire you could have a lot more stuff and you will feel a bit stiffer. So budget for £500 to £1,000.

Then stamp duty. At the moment Stamp Duty Land Tax – to give it its full name – is 1% of the price of any property bought for more than £120,000, up to £250,000. So buying somewhere at £125,000 incurs the full SDLT of 1% on the total. Here is the final sum.

Old home	£250,000
New home	£125,000
Profit	**£125,000**

Expenses

Makeover	£500
Estate agent 2% of old home	£5,000
Solicitor selling and buying	£1,500
Survey on new home	£500
SDLT	£1,250
Move	£1,000
Total	**£9,750**

Net profits £125,000 – £9,750 = £115,250.

So all these expenses have set you back nearly £10,000 – around 8% of the profit you thought you would make. And it will be a bit worse than that after the Home Information Pack starts in 2007. And your £115,000 will buy you a flat-rate pension of around £7,500 a year at 65. Not that much to live on – especially stuck out where your new home is.

Staying put is an alternative. You can do what is called 'equity release', taking value out of your home but still living there. They work like this. You borrow money against the value of your home. While you live, you pay no interest on the loan. Instead, each year (or each month in some cases) the interest due is added to your loan. When you die, the loan and all the accrued interest is taken from your estate. In some cases there will be nothing left of the value of your home. But don't worry, these plans come with a guarantee that the debt will never exceed the value of your home. Nowadays, these schemes are called 'lifetime mortgages'. The problem with them is you will not get that much because the company that makes the loan – or the one that insures the guarantee that the loan will never exceed the value of the property – will want to minimise their risk. A loan of £30,000 at an interest rate of 6.5% (which is fairly typical, the rates tend to be higher than normal mortgages) will grow to around £77,000 in 15 years, and at 65 most people will expect to live rather more than that. So don't expect to be able to get a loan of much more than a third of the value of your home – and do expect to pay about £1,000 in fees. And £77,000 will buy you a flat-rate pension at 65 of about £5,100.

The other sort of equity release is slightly different. There is no loan. Instead, the company buys the property from you, giving you the right to live there. Again, do not expect that much. At 70 – it is hard to do it any younger – expect about 40% of the value. So on your £250,000 home you would get £100,000. It sounds a lot, but over your expected life of 15 years it is 100,000/15 = £6,666. And if you buy an annuity you will get around £8,300 a year.

So unless you have several houses or a whopping great mansion, your home is not going to be your pension. At least, not if you want it to provide a really good pension. See p. 155 for more on buying to let if you really want to pursue this idea.

I DON'T PLAN TO WORK HERE LONG

This is the most pathetic excuse for not joining a company pension scheme. Even if you work there for as little as three months – and it is not really a career enhancer to work somewhere for less than that – you can keep the value of your pension, including all the money your employer and the Chancellor have put in, and transfer it to another scheme. For example, you join plewis.biz and earn £30,000 a year as an assistant web designer (if you look at www.plewis.biz, you will see it has been done by a very assistant web designer). Your employer offers you a company pension scheme where you put in up to 5% of your gross pay, he (for it is a he) matches it and of course the Chancellor allows both of you to pay no tax on any of this. So when you leave after two years there is £6,000 in there, which has cost you as a basic-rate taxpayer just £2,340. Net profit £3,760. For doing no work. Now OK, you have to transfer this money to another pension scheme and of course it will be tied up for the foreseeable future and you have no idea what pension it will buy you at 65 or whenever you retire, but hey – it is there and it is yours, it has your name and National Insurance number on it. A handsome £3,000 from plewis.biz and £760 from the Chancellor, gift-wrapped. Now, if you turned this down, you will have had £2,340 more in your pay packet but you will have no money in your pension, your employer will have saved £3,000 and the Chancellor will be £760 better off.

So if you join a company that offers a pension scheme which the employer pays into, **JOIN IT**. If you don't, you are volunteering for a pay cut.

The half sister to this pathetic excuse is 'I may not stay here more than a few years and I expect to move around a lot during my career'. Well bully for you. We all expect that nowadays. The days of a job for life and pension and gold watch after 40 years' service are long gone. But it is not an excuse for not joining the company scheme. Unless you leave in less than three months, in which case you will get back the contributions you have paid in yourself but **not** those paid in by your employer and the Chancellor will deduct the extra he chipped in too. So you haven't lost anything. But if you leave after three months, you have two choices. Only they are sort of dressed up as *several* choices. So let's go through them.

After you have paid into a pension scheme for a certain length of time, you have a right to that pension which cannot be taken away. At that point, they say your rights are 'vested'. Your rights have to be 'vested' by law after you've paid in for at least two years, but some schemes will vest them after a shorter time – sometimes as little as 12 months. Once your rights have vested, the two choices are:

1. you can leave the money in the company's pension pot and let it grow there. Nothing more will be added, but when you reach 65 you can then take that fund and buy yourself a pension – or indeed do whatever the rules allow you to when you reach that age.
2. you can take what is called a 'transfer value', which is the value of everything put into the fund and all the growth, less the charges, and move it to another pension – either another company scheme or a personal pension of your own.

If you leave *before* your rights have 'vested' but *after* the three-month period when all you can do is take back your own contributions, you have two other choices. Either you can be really, really stupid and pretend you have only been there a few weeks and take back your contributions, letting the company and the Chancellor reclaim what they paid in . . . .or you can be sensible and take the value of your pension (roughly speaking what you, your employer and the Chancellor have paid in) and move it to another pension scheme. That other scheme could be with a new employer or be a personal pension of your own.

In short, even if you move jobs a lot in a fluid, go-getting kind of way, you still have no excuse for not paying into a company pension.

I'M SAVING UP ALREADY!

Good. Saving is important (but see **Cutting Debt** on p. 147). But saving for a pension has advantages. When you save for a pension through a pension scheme of some sort, every penny you put in comes out of your income **before** you pay tax on it. What that means is that if you pay £100 into your pension scheme, the Revenue gives you back the tax you have paid on it. If you are a basic rate taxpayer that means for every £100 you put in, you get an extra £28.20 from the taxman. Why £28.20? Add £100 and £28.20. That gives £128.20. Then work out the tax on that at the basic rate, which is 22%: £128.20 × 0.22 = £28.20. So the taxman is restoring the money you have paid already in tax. There are two further bits of good news. It does not matter if you pay tax at the lower rate of 10% or even pay no tax at all, you can get tax relief on your pension contributions at the basic rate. And it is even better news for richer folk. If you pay higher-rate tax, and about three and a half million people in the UK do, then the taxman is much more generous. Instead of adding £28.20 to your hundred quid you will get a massive £66.67. Again, work it out: £166.67 × 0.4 = £66.67 which means to have £100 in your pocket you must have earned £166.67. So the best-off eighth of the working population gets more than double the tax relief per hundred pounds they pay. This tax relief does not come cheap. As we saw earlier, tax relief costs at least £12.3 billion a year (and arguably double that) and most of that – about 55% – goes to higher-rate taxpayers.

One justification for doing it like this is that when the money is paid out as a pension, three quarters of it has to be used to buy an income of some sort and that money is taxed. So although it is tax free on the way in, most of it is taxed on the way out. That is doubly valuable. First, it means there is more money going into your fund from the start and all that will have many years to grow. Second, the chances are that in retirement you will pay a lower rate of tax – and certainly not a higher one unless you are very lucky – so the tax relief on the way in will probably be worth more (and certainly not less) than the tax on the income you draw in retirement. That is borne out by the figures that show that the cost of tax relief on money being saved up for a pension is more than double the tax which is actually paid on pensions. Partly of course because you can draw a quarter of your fund tax free. So tax free on the way in and on the way out.

All this means that the tax advantages of saving up for a pension are huge. Of course there are other tax-free ways of saving. Money put into an Individual Savings Account (ISA) grows tax free, and when you take the money out it is also tax free. However, money you put in has to come out of your taxed income. In other words, when you put £100 in you have already paid tax on it and have had to earn £128.20 (actually £151.50 when you count National Insurance contributions, and more still – £169.49 – if you are a higher-rate taxpayer including National Insurance contributions) to put that money away.

So the money in ISAs is taxed on the way in and tax free on the way out. That means you don't have the advantage of the tax relief in the fund and growing. And when you use the money in retirement, the money you take out is tax free but that may well be when you are paying a lower rate of tax. There are also tough restrictions on how much you put into an ISA. At the best it is £7,000 a year – and only £3,000 into a cash ISA rather than an investment ISA. Although that is rather more than most people put into their pension (£7000 a year is £583 a month), it can still be a limitation compared to the new freedom and flexibility which pension investments allow. So all in all ISAs are not as tax efficient or as useful as pensions. But they do have one big advantage: you can take the money out whenever you need it. A pension fund has to stay there until you are at least 55 (until 2010 that age is 50) and you are constrained in what you can do with the money. An ISA is yours to take out and squander whenever you please.

So the ideal state is where you put loads into your pension and loads more into your ISA. But not everyone can do that. And the same amount of money put into an ISA will not grow as quickly as put into a pension, because there is no tax relief boost at the start.

IT'S TOO LONG OFF TO WORRY ABOUT

This objection is normally coupled with, 'the world will be a very different place then' – which is slightly more sensible in that it is true, whereas 'too long off to worry about' is not true. Or you might think, 'Oh sod it, I'll be dead then. Why should I worry?'

So why did you buy this book?

'I didn't, I was given it.'

OK, but you have read this far rather than chucking it away.

'It's something to do. I was bored.'

Come off it. No-one's life is so boring that the best option is to read a book about pensions. Even an entertaining one like this. No. The truth is you have read it this far and that means you are a bit worried. If you are really not, then fine, close it now. I make money from people buying it, not reading it. But when you are 65 and have very little money, remember back and think, 'God if I had read *Live Long and Prosper* a bit more carefully, I might not be in such a mess'. I don't care. By then I shall be long gone. But you might have 30 years of life, if you can call it that, on £114 a week. Actually I do care – I don't want that for anyone. It is why I wrote this book and why, I hope, you're reading it.

The truth is that life passes very quickly. And planning when you are young can save pining when you are old. The one objection that may have some truth in it is that the world – and pensions – will be very different then. Thirty years ago they were different and 30 years before that they were very different again. But one thing remains true. However many changes the world undergoes, the people with money cope with them better than the people without. The detail may change but that truth does not. And don't give me any crap about not surviving. Today's adults will live longer, healthier lives than any humans in history. And if you are fitter and more aware for longer, it will only make the pain of poverty that much more apparent. Deep breath. Lecture over. On to the next objection. And please don't say you'd rather go clubbing.

I'D RATHER GO CLUBBING . . .

What did I say? Do not even think about it. Your own future is much more important.

OK, I can see that isn't enough. Why should it be? Clubbing or sailing or buying stuff or going on that second holiday a year or, for heaven's sake, just looking after the kids and feeding them well, mean you simply don't have enough to save for a pension.

For some people that is a fair option – but let me tell you what will happen if you don't save. Britain is a civilised society. We don't let our old people starve to death or die of cold. Do we?

Well, we try not to. Unlike some wealthy countries (actually I can only really think of America), we don't let people have no money. And once you reach 60 the state will step in and give you money to make up your weekly income to £114.05 a week if you are single. Or £174.05 if you are a couple – that's between you, by the way, not each. In addition it will pay your rent and council tax. And everyone over 60 gets free prescriptions and free or half-price public transport. So you can live, but it is not easy. To see how hard it might be, write down your take-home pay per month now. That's the bottom line, the one that actually gets paid into your bank each month by your employer. Take off your housing costs – rent or mortgage and council tax – because the state will give you those too (not your mortgage, but by then you won't have one) then multiply that by 12 to give the annual amount of money you have to spend. Compare that with what the state will give you – £5,930 if you are single or £9,050 if you are a couple (that's £4,525 each).

At this point the readers divide into two groups. One lot thinks, 'Bloody hell! If I do nothing I will have to live on less than a quarter (or a fifth or a tenth) of what I do now. Please, please tell me how to avoid that fate.'

The other half will think, 'Actually, that's about half of what I have now. And half my income is about what most pensions aim to pay. So there's no point in making those sacrifices and saving.' You might want to read the rest of the book. Especially the chapter on the state pension which explains what you might get in a bit more detail. Or you might pass it on to a friend who earns more. No, come to think of it, let them buy one . . . they can afford to.

. . . OR BUY A HOUSE

Just in time. 'I can't afford it. I have a mortgage and family to pay for' is a reason for not putting money into a pension that is very hard for me to object to. And it is closely related to

I've got debt so I shouldn't pay into a pension

You've clearly been reading other things I have written. It is a sensible objection and one that needs very careful thought. Such careful thought that there is a whole chapter devoted to it – and the priority of buying a house. See Chapter 8, Debt and Houses.

> ### Rule of Prosperity
>
> **Nothing else is as good as a pension when it comes to saving for a pension.**

CHAPTER THREE

Live Long and Prosper? The real causes of the pensions crisis

CRISIS . . .

Actually by saying that – the real causes of the pensions crisis – I am begging the question ('in the correct sense of the word to mean that I assume there *is* a crisis, not the sloppy sense frequently used even by people at the BBC who should know better when they mean 'that raises the question').

So let's ask that begged question first. Is there a pensions crisis? If you ask government ministers they will tell you that there is not one now. But there would be one in 20 years or so if we made no changes to the way pensions are organised in the UK (and I use the word 'organised' loosely). That is why the Government set up a major enquiry: the Pensions Commission was appointed in 2003 and its job is 'To keep under review the regime for UK private pensions and long-term savings'. More of that – and the Commission – later, though it is worth saying that just because the Government appointed a high-powered commission and put all change on hold until it reported in 2005, it doesn't mean there will be a pensions crisis. Indeed, the word is carefully avoided in the 350 pages of the Commission's first report, called by the upbeat sub-title 'Challenges and Choices' rather than the more dramatic 'Crisis and Panic'.

Government ministers seem virtually alone in believing that a crisis in pensions is not here already, or at least knocking on our door. The press certainly thinks so. The phrase 'pensions crisis' appeared 1,100 times – three times every day – in the UK's daily and Sunday newspapers in 2005. In 2001, it had appeared just 21 times all year.

The elements of the crisis are usually stated as increasing life expectancy, falling birth rates, poorly-performing investments in pension funds, new regulation which makes company pensions more expensive and their costs more apparent, the rising cost of public sector pensions and the unwillingness to save among many younger people. Finding a solution to this crisis is made harder by the 'bewildering complexity' of 'the most complex pension system in the world' (to quote the Pensions Commission).

But for once I am sort of going to side with the Government. There is no pensions crisis *as of now* (American phrases like that give a wonderful seriousness to a simple thought). In other words, today's pensioners are on the whole better off than they have ever been. And yes I know a lot are still very hard up, but a guaranteed income of £114.05 plus council tax is a lot more than the poorest pensioners have had in the past. Yes, the system is complex and two million who could claim Pension Credit or council tax benefit do not do so, but it is there for those who want to. And just to take the Government's side again briefly, it is working hard on the pesky problem of the low take-up of means-tested benefits. It will never solve it but it could improve.

There are big deficits in salary-related company pension schemes. But they are being reduced by a combination of big extra contributions by the companies – soon to be forced on them by the fierce new Pensions Regulator – and a stock market which rose by around 40% in the last three years. Although most salary-related pension schemes are closed to new members, many others are not and 3.6 million employees of private sector companies are still covered by salary-related pensions. Although money-purchase schemes are not so good, they do at least get money from employers saved up for use in the future.

Sorry to use some technical terms there – see Chapter 5 for a full explanation of these different pension schemes.

In the public sector, the costs of pensions adds around £18 billion a year onto the taxes paid by everyone. With the number of people employed by the public sector growing strongly and what they are paid rising faster than it is in the private sector, the future cost could be quite alarming. And the cost will not be helped by the Government's decision in 2005 to allow all civil servants, health-service workers and teachers who start their jobs before the summer of 2006 to retain their retirement age of 60.

> The Government is not so much acting like King Canute, who sat on the beach in his throne to prove even a king couldn't stop the tide, but more like those well-meaning folk who built flood defences on the Norfolk coast only to discover that they just moved the problem elsewhere. In Norfolk they have now adopted a new policy: don't build the defences, and let the homes fall into the sea as the sandy cliffs they stand on are eroded by the waves. The poor homeowners of littoral Norfolk are not paid any compensation for this change of heart. How different it is with pensions. The Government is just beginning to let the rising tide of life expectancy erode the length of our retirement. But it is making sure that, among its own employees anyway, there are no losers.

Around half the workforce – maybe 12 million people – do not have a pension scheme to join and of those who do, an estimated three million do not bother. That problem may be tackled by the Government in the future if it follows the advice of Lord Turner: then every employer should pay in to some sort of pension scheme and all employees should be automatically enrolled in it though they will be able to pull out if they want to. The details of any changes are still being worked out and it will be some years before any change begins.

Life expectancy is growing faster than experts predicted and actuaries now accept there may be no biological limit to how far that process will go. At the same time the birth rate is declining, and immigration is not going to fill the gap. So the ratio of workers to retired people is going to fall as the middle of the century approaches. There is only one solution to this problem – those who are going to live longer will have to spend some of that extra time working.

So it is good that the Pensions Commission has put forward the stark message that we have to save more, work longer, pay more tax, or be poorer. One way or another the problems have to get severe enough for a future government to accept that and raise not just the state pension age above 65 – which would give a powerful signal – but, as the UK's largest employer, also raise the age at which pensions are paid to the five million people whose salaries and pensions are paid for by the public, you and me, out of our taxes.

. . . WHAT CRISIS?

tomorrow's company – and you can tell it is a look-ahead kind of place because it doesn't use capital letters in its name – reckons there is no future problem about affording pensions, despite the fears about the dependency ratio. Its report says there isn't a savings gap. Well I agree there. It says, 'it is impossible to forecast accurately what society will look like in 30 to 40 years'. That is also clearly true (who could have predicted the ringtone business – and that it would outstrip pop singles – in 1966? And of course who could have predicted the lengthening of human life in 1976? Not actuaries certainly). It says there isn't a problem about the dependency ratio. Mmm. Not so sure about that. But here is how the argument goes. First, it doesn't accept that ratio that Turner and others use. So much for Adair T's hopes that his first report would be an 'undebateable set out of the facts'. The debate began before his second report was at the printer.

If you recall that bit about the dependency ratio, you will also recall that Lord Turner of Ecchinswell, as he now is (the peerage came between the last chapter and this), used what I called a 'rough and ready' measure of the dependency ratio – the number of people aged 20–64 over the number of people aged below 20 and 65 plus. Now that ignores two important things (three, if you count the fact that there are quite a number of people under 20 who work). First is the fact that 9 million people under the age of 65 do not do paid work.

Many of them of course bring up children or care for sick or disabled people and that saves the state money and prepares a future generation for work. So it is work of tremendous value but it does not directly contribute to the economy now – so these people should be on the 'dependent' side of the ratio. Second, more than a million people over the age of 65 still work. And that number is set to more than double over the next few years (yes I know that's a vague statement; it came from a survey by an insurance company that used the results to try to sell us more stuff now. But it is almost certainly on the right lines). So some people under 65 who Turner counts as 'supporters' are dependants, and a growing number above that age who Turner reckons are 'dependants' are not.

tomorrow's company (and thank goodness its modernism doesn't extend to eschewing apostrophes) says that taking account of these things changes the dependency ratio considerably. I won't go into the more recondite detail as I am in no position to referee a contest between tomorrow's company and The Pensions Commission. But the economists who did the report for tomorrow's company also fiddle a bit more with the figures to produce another new idea, a 'total economic support ratio', which it says was 0.48 in 2003 and would fall to 0.45 by 2041 – which is almost the same as it was in 1961. So no problem. Or at least as little problem as we had in 1961. Now if you are scratching your head as my editor was at this point, **don't worry**. The total economic support ratio is a bit like the dependency ratio – the differences don't matter. What matters is that it will be much the same in 2041 as it was in 1961.

Sadly though, I might point out that 1961 was the year in which the first attempt was made to solve a future pensions crisis with the introduction of the graduated pension which most people retiring today have. It is based on contributions they paid between 1961 and 1975 and pays newly retired people on average £1.69 a week each (which is in fact £3.55 for men and £0.59 for women). So it was not a great solution, especially for women. But maybe not a great crisis either. At least no worse than it will be in 2041. According to tomorrow's company.

Underneath all this though is something very important. There are more people in work, as the Labour Government will tell you endlessly, 'than ever'. Many of those are working wives who in the past would have treated marriage as a period of not so much unpaid holiday as of unpaid domestic service (thank God that has changed). And a fair number more are those over pension age who want to and choose to work and manage to find a job. So tomorrow's company's message – and the report is 56 pages long – is that we needn't worry about the declining number of people supporting the holidays of the retired. First, the ratio of workers to holidaymakers isn't declining as much as we fear (see above) and second, those in work will be so much more productive in future that whatever gap remains will close. 'Productive' here broadly means the amount of economic growth we give for every hour spent at work. So more of us will work, and while we are there, we will produce more wealth.

So there you are. It doesn't matter, it's not a crisis and we needn't worry.

In a way of course I hope tomorrow's company is right. We won't know for a long time. And doing nothing is always an option when a problem seems too difficult to deal with. But even if it is right, saving more and taking steps now won't make things any worse in 2041, and will almost certainly make them better.

HOW WE GOT HERE

You could blame high levels of unemployment in the 1980s. A generation ago the talk was all of early retirement, as the government brought unemployment down by encouraging employers to get rid of anyone over 50 so younger people could have at least half a chance of getting a job. The over 50s were encouraged to retire early by offering them much the same pensions from their jobs as they would have had at 60 or even 65. Private employers paid for this policy out of their bulging pension funds, boosted to embarrassing levels after years of solid stock market growth. And of course where the public sector was the employer, then taxpayers paid the bill, or promised to, without even realising it.

As the middle-aged left their jobs, more young people did get work and unemployment fell. The cost was pushed into the future. Which is now. And we are paying it – not only in the deficits of pensions funds and the huge and growing cost of public-sector pensions, but in the raised expectations that as the country got more prosperous we would all be able to retire earlier, just at the time we were all living longer. So the start of the great late paid holiday was brought forward five or even ten years by early retirement, just as the end was being delayed five or more years by increasing longevity. As David Blunkett said while he was the Secretary of State for Work and Pensions – we want to retire earlier, live longer and have someone else pay for it.

The present generation of young pensioners are better off, and retired earlier, than is going to be possible for the rest of us. The struggle now is to make sure that we can hope to retire at 65 – rather than at 70 or older.

LONGER LIVES

'How long will I live?' It's a question we all ask – or its slightly more depressed version, 'When will I die?' Like anything to do with numbers, there is a simple answer that is approximate and a much more complicated one that heads slowly towards the truth. First, the simple one. If you are an adult under 50 you can expect to live to around 82 if you are a woman or 78 if you're a bloke. If you are in your fifties, add a year. In your sixties, add three and in your seventies, add five or six. Beyond that it gets trickier. Alternatively just write down 120. Because that may be the answer too.

Life expectancy is growing faster than anyone predicted. Every time actuaries look at what it might be in future, it has grown longer. And even though they build that error into today's prediction, next time they look it is longer still. In October 2005 the Government Actuary, the Future Cruncher in Chief, Chris Daykin announced that he had stopped assuming that the length of life had some ultimate biological limit. In other words, the age we live to really could go on increasing forever. Or as he put it in actuary-speak, 'Previous projections have assumed that rates of mortality would gradually diminish in the long term . . . However . . . the previous long-term assumptions have been too pessimistic. Thus . . . the rates of improvement after 2029 are now assumed to remain constant.'

Hang on a minute. What about obesity, bad diet, lack of exercise, smoking, drugs, pollution, all that stuff which is really bad for us? Doesn't that mean that today's younger generation will actually live a shorter time; that their life expectancy will be less than that of today's older generation? After all, the oldies were brought up in the pollution-free times of World War II and, despite all that privation, research has shown that they ate a really healthy diet. So as long as the bombs missed them, the rest of their life was coasting.

Well, no. Despite these concerns about our unhealthy lifestyle, life expectancy only goes one way – up. And the Government Actuary's sentence quoted above represents one of the biggest changes in actuarial practice for 200 years.

ACTUARIAL WITH THE TRUTH

The actuarial profession began in England in the 18th century with people grubbing round graveyards writing down how old people were when they died (in fact the first attempts were made a century earlier using German mortality records because they wrote them down on paper which we did not. But no-one knew if they would be the same as in England, so here they donned their boots and headed for the cemetery). Mathematicians soon realised that the age of death could be analysed just like any other set of numbers. And that the rate of death followed rules. This angered Christians who thought that death was in the gift of God, not mathematicians (which was of course before many people realised that mathematicians were God and if there is any ultimate truth it is to be found in numbers).

The men who ran insurance companies were happy enough to attend church on Sunday but during the week they used this new godless tool to make money. Instead of assessing every individual who came before them for life insurance – which believe it or not is what they used to do – they just played the odds. The maths said that out of any population so many would be dead by the age of 50, so many more by 60, so many more by 70 and so on. Fix the premiums accordingly and with a large enough number of customers, the chance visits of the grim reaper would ensure they always made a profit. Although insurance sales reps are dressed in more sober clothes than the croupier's in the local casino, the maths they use is essentially the same – indeed it started in the gambling dens of the 17th century. The only real difference is that gambling is fun so people will pay what is asked. But buying insurance is so dull that people want to get it over as quickly as they can. So they can go to the casino and enjoy themselves.

But a problem was soon discovered and it still exists. The people who take out long-term insurance products live longer than the general population. This is good news for the companies when it comes to life insurance – the longer you live the more premiums they collect before the inevitable payout – but bad news for those that provide pensions and annuities. Because the longer you live the more they pay out. So when you ask 'how long will I live' the answer will depend on whether you have a pension or not. If you do, you will live longer. A lot longer. For example, the Government Actuary projections say that people aged 60 will live about another 20 years – slightly more for a woman, less for a man. But projections done for the life insurance industry using data from their customers published in 2005 reckon that life expectancy at 60 is almost 30 years. Even looked at as a matter of simple arithmetic, the cost of a pension over 30 years is half as much again as a pension paid over 20 years. Of course, the arithmetic is never simple when it comes to pensions. First, the value now of a pension paid over 30 years is worth less than half as much again as one paid over 20 years. It is in fact only about a third more because the payments paid into the future are worth less and less in today's terms.

But there is another factor that increases the cost – and that is uncertainty. Two things are uncertain. One is the rate of inflation and the rate of return on investments (that may sound like two things, but what we need is the difference between the two and it is that which is uncertain, even though it is roughly constant in the long run; in the short run it is not). Second, the length of life. We can say half the population will die by a certain date and half will live longer. But that midpoint is itself uncertain, as we have seen. So some money has to be set aside to insure against the uncertainty. And the further we push estimates into the future, the more the uncertainties grow and the more the cost of that uncertainty. We can hope, as we have in other approximations, that these two uncertainties cancel each other out. If so, we can rely on the common-sense view that a pension paid for twice as long is going to cost roughly twice as much. And as long as we don't apply for a job as a pension scheme actuary we can probably get away with it.

So whatever the fine detail of the calculation, the real problem is that a small increase in life expectancy causes a much bigger increase in the cost of pensions. For example, in 1982 a 65 year old man could expect to live a shade under 13 years. Twenty-one years later that had grown to around 16 years and one month, which is an increase of just over three years. But it represents a rise of almost a quarter in the length of his retirement and thus (almost) a quarter in the cost of paying his pension. So if the contributions were fixed in 1980, by the time he retires in 2002 there will be a quarter too little in the pot to pay the pension promised.

A lot of rather silly claims are made for the increase in life expectancy over the last hundred years. You will read that when the first old age pension was introduced, it began at 70 and life expectancy was only 48. Well, that *is* true in a way. If you were born around the start of the 20th century, life expectancy was indeed mid forties. But once you had reached 65, you had a reasonable expectation of another decade.

In 1908 when the first state pension was paid – though only at 70 – a man of 65 could expect to live until he was nearly 76, a woman until she was 77. By 1928, when the pension age was reduced to 65, life expectancy had grown by about 6 months for men and a year for women. The pension age for women was reduced to 60 from 1948 and by then a 65 year old woman could expect to live to 80 and a man to

77½. When Barbara Castle introduced SERPS in 1978 men's expectation was much the same but for women it had grown another year. Today the figures are 81½ and nearly 84½ .

Now before we leave actuary school, one thing remains. When will you die? I got rather obsessed with this while writing the book (the answer for me is depressingly soon) and you can find out your big day from our website (I was going to call it your 'dig day' but as most people are cremated nowadays that didn't quite work). Put in your birth date and it will tell you your expected date of death, as well as how many days you have lived and how many are left to you. Forget your 30th birthday or your half century, what about celebrating your 10,000th day or indeed your 20,000th?

There is such uncertainty about the figures that they are relatively meaningless anyway. But for some reason everyone I have tried it out on finds it fun. In a macabre sort of way. The figures used are all UK figures from the Government Actuary tables for 2002–2004 which were published on 10 November 2005. Of course health, genes, country of birth, occupation, sex (no-one knows if more or less makes any difference, but male or female definitely does), smoking (all bad), other drug habits (probably on the bad side), alcohol (a bit good, a lot bad), diet, body/mass index (more than 25 bad, more than 30 very bad) all move you away from the average in one direction or the other. Just to give two examples, people in Scotland die younger on the whole than people in the rest of the UK. You can subtract a couple of years if you are Scottish. And of course smokers die younger on the whole than non-smokers – deduct five or six years.

At this point the smokers who like pub quizzes will be thinking, 'What about Jeanne Calment?' She was the Frenchwoman who died at the record age of 122 in 1997 in Arles in southwest France and could remember meeting van Gogh in her mother-in-law's shop. And she smoked. Two things to say about Mme Calment. First, she gave up smoking at 120: it's never too late. And second, if she hadn't smoked she might still be alive today! And next year you will have to choose between smoking and pub quizzes anyway. If the answer is too depressing, remember that the Government Actuary's Department is the most pessimistic of the experts in this field. That is partly because the future crunchers there look at all people (including all those who are clearly not like you and die young) and partly because these figures do not take account of future increases in life expectancy. That can add a couple of years. Finally, these figures were the best estimate for 2003, since when things have moved on. The Continuous Mortality Investigation, which is for 2005 and takes account of future increases in life expectancy and looks at a better-off group, adds about seven years to the GAD figures. Remember too that these ages are the ones by which half the people of your age will have died and half will not. So you have a 50:50 chance (and – bearing everything else in mind – probably rather more) of living longer than this. So if you stick a pin in on that day half the people will react, though some will just think it is time for their injection.

So having got past all the warnings and so on, here is your most likely age at death depending how old you are now.

Age now	Expected age at death	
	Female	Male
25	81y 2m	76y 11m
30	81y 4m	77y 2m
35	81y 5m	77y 5m
40	81y 7m	77y 8m
45	81y 10m	78y 0m
50	82y 2m	78y 6m
55	82y 8m	79y 1m
60	83y 3m	80y 0m
65	84y 1m	81y 2m
70	85y 2m	82y 8m
75	86y 8m	84y 7m
80	88y 8m	87y 2m

If you think this is a bit vague, let me give you an example from the web page at **www.acblack.com/livelongandprosper**. I don't know your birth date so I'll pick one: 14 October 1977. And I'll pick a sex for you: female. And I will assume you are reading this book on the day it is published: 24 April 2006. The calculator will reveal that you are 28 years 192 days old – which is 10,419 days. And you have around 65% of your life left, which is just over 53 years. More precisely there are 19,261 days left before you die on 17 January 2059 at the age of 82. Of course, chances are you won't die on that day – if only life (and death) were that simple. But it is the most likely date of death of all the possibles for people of your exact age in the UK on the date of publication. Frightening. But worse for a bloke: he would die on 5 November 2054.

> ### Rule of Prosperity
>
> **Work longer. Or if you can't face that, die younger. Either way you will have more to spend when you do retire.**

INVESTMENT

The second thing that affects our wealth in retirement (all other things being equal) is how much the money we have saved up for our pension has 'earned'. I put it in inverted commas because I don't really see money as earning anything. It just sits there. We work our butts off; money does nothing. I have a fairly Puritan view of work: work is what we do; it is how we make wealth both for ourselves and for others, and it is really the most worthwhile thing we can do. So the idea of sticking money in a bank or buying shares with it and watching it grow and making me richer, to me borders on the immoral. Pretty close to what others might call sponging (though actually individuals who have no money and do not work and live off the state are really hard up and they have nothing but my sympathy. It is people who do no work and are wealthy that really offend me). But leaving my strange morality aside, how much our pension fund has grown all by itself is a very important factor in how much we will have.

Over the last 50 years the people who run pension funds have believed in the cult of the equity. Now just to explain, it is not really a cult (though belief in it generally borders on the irrational) and the word 'equity' is just a posh word for 'share' (if you want to know about shares see p. 118). So the cult of the equity believes that investing in shares is the best way, some say the only way, to see your money grow. The cult began in the 1950s with a man called George Ross Goobey. He was in charge of the pension fund at Imperial Tobacco. Half a century ago the few company pension schemes that existed invested their money in government stock and bonds. These investments pay a guaranteed amount at a fixed time and are an ideal investment for pension funds because, guess what, a salary-related pension does exactly the same. Each member will retire on a definite date and will be earning a fairly predictable amount. So it seems sensible to match the investment to the liability. But Ross Goobey noticed that government bonds produced a return of about 3% a year of the amount invested and shares were returning about 4% a year, mainly through the dividends they paid. So why not move the fund into shares? That way it would grow more quickly and would require lower contributions to meet the pension promises.

Other employers followed suit, saving themselves money and promising in return that if the pension fund did not grow enough – because share returns, although bigger, did carry that risk – they would make up the difference. There was of course only one winner of this change. The employer. The employees did not get any more pension when they retired. They just got the pension that had been promised. But the employer paid less for it. The gamble was that the fund would grow enough on those lower contributions to meet the pension promise. If it didn't the employer would make up the difference.

There was another big advantage too. It also saved money now and pushed the risk well into the future. As we have seen elsewhere in this book, the present value of paying someone £100 today is £100. But the value now of promising to pay someone £100 in ten years is a lot less. In fact about £78, assuming the real return on money is around

2.5% a year and not taking account of the chance they will die meanwhile. Which is the numerical version of the old saying 'a bird in the
hand is worth two in the bush' – which is true when the bush is about
24 years away.

So George RG had little trouble persuading the board of Imperial
Tobacco to let him move the whole of the fund out of bonds and into
shares. At the time these decisions, although nominally taken by
trustees, were in effect taken by the company. After all it had to keep
the pension promise. And the trustees tended to be some of the company's directors. Other companies soon noticed that Imperial Tobacco
was paying less into its pension fund than they were. They looked at
the arguments. It was a win-win situation, so they made the change
too. And within a few years pension funds were largely invested in
shares. And for 50 years it seemed an excellent policy. Even at times of
high inflation – which peaked in the UK at 26.9% a year in August
1975 – the overall return on shares held up. For the last quarter of the
last century, money invested in shares rose by 12% a year. In other
words, it doubled every six years.

That's not to say there wasn't some caution among fund managers.
After all if they just put the money in shares there would be little
for them to do. So they put some in riskier things like commercial
property, some in really wild stuff like shares in other countries
(gosh) and a chunk in those safe old dull-but-guaranteed bonds.
Generally around three quarters of the money was in shares –
mainly UK – and a quarter was mainly in bonds with a bit in property for good measure (and to keep the fund managers earning
their large salaries).

Wind on to the year 2000. As the new century dawned, brows were
wiped and 'phews' exchanged when the millennium bug scam was
finally rumbled. (Or rather it wasn't, it just didn't happen. People who
had spent vast amounts on solving a problem that didn't exist of
course justified the cost on grounds of risk protection. My suspicions
that the whole thing was not quite what it seemed were confirmed
when one of the biggest publicists of the problems, and how his com-

pany could solve them, began to miss interviews on the grounds that he was in South Africa choosing the vineyard he was going to buy in early 2000). But just as that problem melted away, it soon became clear that all was not well with shares. The price of them began to fall. And fall. Rise a bit. And fall. And fall. And fall. It was then I coined the phrase, 'Remember, share prices can fall, as well as plummet'. And plummet they did. Through 2000, 2001 (and don't tell me about the terrorist attack on New York and Washington: following 11 September 2001 share prices in London fell over the next eight trading days but then rose and by 5 October they were back where they were on 10 September, and the underlying downward path soon began again. You have to wonder what you need to do to the USA to cause a real stock market effect), 2002 and for the first couple of months of 2003. By 12 March that year they reached their low point and slowly began to rise. They ended 2003 13.6% higher than they started it and grew another 7.5% in 2004, followed by a third year when they ended 2005 up by nearly 17% .

I give you all these figures to explain something weird. Between their peak on the last day of the old century on 31 December 1999 to their nadir on 12 March 2003, the index that measures share prices fell from 6,930 to 3,287. You can see that 3,287 is less than half 6,930 and in fact share prices fell by around 53%. Since that low point the index has risen by 75%. So share prices should be more than back to where they were, shouldn't they? No. Sorry that is not true. If something is worth £1,000 and its value falls by 50%, half, it is worth. . . .

Yes, £500. If its value then grows by 50% it is worth. . . .

Yes £750, which is £500 + half of £500, which is £250.

To grow back after a fall of 50% a price has to grow by. . . .

Yes, 100% . If it halves one way it has to double the other. And we are not there yet – not by a long way.

So even after three years of steady growth, share prices are now still worth about 25% less than when they were at their peak as the 21st century dawned.

> OK, OK. Some of you – not many but enough – are thinking 'what is this ignoramus going on about? The 21st century started on 1 January 2001, not 1 January 2000. There was no year nought, so the first century began on 1/1/01 and the 19th century began 1900 years later on 1/1/1901 and the present century kicked off on 1/1/2001'. The logic is hard to fault. But all this counting stuff is just what people do. And the century, still more the millennium, really arrives when all the numbers change. It is that magic moment when we go from 1999 to 2000. So that's when I am talking about.

In fact if you invested in shares about seven years ago, you would just about have the same amount now as you had then. So zero percent return a year. You'd have done better with your money in a bank account. A lot better in some bank accounts. The result is that many pension fund managers have earned their money by moving investments out of the stock market and into safe things, like bonds. Not all of it but a big proportion. The result is that the investment in shares has fallen from around 70–75% to perhaps 50–60%. No-one really knows – they are all very cagey. And as shares start rising again, the cult of the equity will grow. Just as end-of-the-world cults grow as centuries come to an end.

One pension fund took a different decision. Over the 15 months to July 2001, the entire £2.3 billion pension fund of the high street chemist Boots plc was moved out of shares and into bonds. This was not a response to the falling stock market – the plummet had hardly begun when the first shares were sold – it was based on the realisation that the size of the fund and the guaranteed return on bonds meant Boots could meet its pension promises without taking any risk. There was enough money, so why bother gambling it on the stock market? Today the price of shares is about 13% lower than the price Boots got. But the return on bonds has been around 3% a year. By May 2004 its pension fund had grown to £2.8 billion, but the Boots board – after many personnel changes – reversed the decision to keep it exclusively in risk-free bonds and put 15% of it back into shares. The pension scheme members of course gained nothing from this change. They still had the promise to pay their salary-related pensions. In effect the shareholders were gambling with the pension fund, hoping they would get a better return in future. At the same time the board announced it would give back £700 million to its shareholders. I wonder why.

POLITICS

Now there are a couple of political points to make. In the red corner is Bruiser Brown, pension scheme raider. And in the blue corner is Liberating Lawson, the company tax slasher. We start with the blue. Appointed as Chancellor in 1983, Lawson began to lay into taxes, delivering body blows to corporate taxes to bring them down and then recovering the tax lost by extending VAT. But the booming economy meant that pension funds were making money hand over fist as stock market growth left them with large surpluses. Or at least actuaries said they had more money than they needed to meet the pension promises they had made. 'Ho ho ho,' they thought, 'isn't the cult of the equity great?'

Better still they could use the pension fund for a bit of a scam. They overpaid into their pension funds – the overpayment being tax free – and that stored up a surplus they could take back in future when times were hard. All the time that companies were heavily taxed, allowing a few tax avoidance perks was just the way the game worked. But Lawson wanted a fair fight. If he slashed company taxes, he was going to keep up his guard on the tax loopholes. And one easy one was using pensions as tax avoidance scams (pronounced 'schemes'). So in 1987 Nigella's Dad (for it was he) introduced a rule that if a pension fund was bigger than it needed to be, the scheme had to take action to reduce the surplus to no more than 5%. The most popular way to do this was to stop paying in – called taking a 'contribution holiday'. And because lots of funds had surpluses far bigger than 5%, lots of firms did just that. Since then the Revenue says nearly £30 billion has officially been kept back from pension funds. Most of it, just over £19 billion, has been taken back by employers either through contribution holidays, cuts in contributions or just taking money out of the scheme. Just over £9 billion has been used to boost pensioners' benefits and another billion or so has been cut from the contributions paid by the employees themselves. Same pension, but costing less.

Ten years later Gordon Brown stepped out of the red corner as the modernising Chancellor of the new Labour government. He also wanted to batter down the taxes companies paid, and he slashed corporation tax. But he also decided that the way companies were taxed was so complex it reduced their incentives to invest. So he changed the way that dividends paid on shares were taxed. That had the effect of taking away the tax refunds on dividends which pension funds enjoyed. Brown insisted it was not the purpose of the change, and if companies saved money as a result they could put it back into their pension funds if they had to. Ha ha. The total cost to pension funds and others of the change to the tax on dividends was £5.4 billion – a year. Brown's first stealth tax. Recent estimates however indicate that the true cost to pension funds was much less – between £2.5 and £3.5 billion a year, and that figure reduces over time. Nevertheless it is a big chunk of money and, nine years on, it is not clear if it has yet exceeded the £30 billion which Nigel Lawson allowed companies to siphon off.

So at the moment it is a draw. But the fight has left pension funds £50 to £60 billion worse off than they would have been if neither policy change had been introduced. And that would go half-way to wiping out the total deficit on the UK's salary-related pension funds.

One final word on 'contribution holidays'. It is not just the politicians that are to blame. We know from official figures that around £30 billion has been withheld from funds because of the laws introduced by Nigel Lawson. But before those laws came in – and even now in some other circumstances – more was held back by companies taking a contribution holiday off their own bat. No-one bothered to count that. So we do not know how much it was or how much bigger it has made the deficits now.

It's time for a little lecture. Most pension funds are (or at least were when all these problems arose) invested in shares. Now what is the one thing to remember about shares?

'Their value can go down as well as plummet?'

Ah, bless you, you have been concentrating. Yes that is important. But it is not quite the **most** important thing. Try again.

'They are volatile?'

Yes. The price can go up and down unpredictably. So what sort of investment are they?

'Er. Uncertain?'

Think more about time. . . .

'Oh I know. Long term!'

Yes! They are a long-term investment. We know that over a period of 100 years or more they always go up. Actually we have only watched them over one period of 100 years and it was true then, but even over periods of 25 years they are pretty certain to out-perform other investments. Though if that is true, why is it that really wealthy families over the long-term – you know, dynastic stuff (HM the Queen, the Duke of Westminster etc) – have prop-erty rather than shares? Perhaps that is the secret they keep from the rest of us and why they are really wealthy dynastic families. Anyway. Shares are for the long term. Over a short period, even ten years or more, they can go down or even, as you so wittily observed, plummet. As they did in 2000–03. Which means that you have to let them rise in the good times so they can absorb the fall (sorry, plummet) in the bad. Nigella's Dad did the opposite. Terrified of a tax scam, his new law meant that as soon as a pension fund had 105% of what it needed – according to actuaries – to meet its pension promises, it had to reduce it. And ten years later Gordon, no doubt noticing that in the previous three years companies had been able to withhold nearly £3.5 billion from their pension funds on that basis, thought he could get away with a major change in taxation painlessly. They were both crass interventions. Because investments in shares are for the long term and if the huge gains of the last quarter of the last century had been left intact we would not be in this mess now.

FAIRNESS

There have been other interventions which have bled away the money in pension funds. At one time pension funds were there to encourage employees to stay with their employer. They were part of what the wittily entitled Human Resources departments call 'recruitment, motivation, retention' of staff. In other words, a good pension encourages people to apply for jobs, makes them work harder while they are there ('no I don't understand this middle one either) and stops them leaving for a company without a pension scheme. Except there isn't much evidence now that it does. But in the past this was used as the excuse for spending the money the schemes cost. So it seemed reasonable then that anyone who left the company – and the scheme – should not have those benefits. Until 1975, if you left your pension scheme before you retired you got nothing back at all except the contributions you had paid in (less tax because of course you had got tax relief when you paid them, so it was recouped by taxing them when you took them back). The fund kept the money your contributions had earned during those years, plus the contributions paid in by the employer. Unravelling that would have been difficult and anyway the employer did not put in a fixed amount relating to you, they just put in what the actuaries told them they had to. So funds gained a lot from early leavers.

From April 1975 schemes were obliged to give people who stayed for at least five years what are called 'preserved rights'. In other words you could leave your contributions in a pension fund, even if you moved to another company. You could not add to them, but you retained the right to draw your pension when you finally reached the scheme's pension age. Of course that was a long time in the future and your pension would relate to your salary when you left your job, so it would not be very much. Another gain to the fund.

Then on 1 January 1986, anyone who left with at least five years in a fund was given a new choice. They could take the value of their pension rights with them. It was called a 'transfer value' and it could be transferred to another pension scheme. Either a personal pension or, if your new employer would accept the transfer – and some won't, into that employer's scheme.

A couple of years later, in April 1988, the five-year period was cut to two years. And from April 2006, as part of the A-Day changes, the two-year wait has been cut to just three months. So that removes almost all the gains for pension funds from early leavers.

Over the same period, the value of any preserved pension you left in a scheme has been increased by changes in the law. Until 1978, the pension you left preserved in a scheme did not have to rise between when you left and when you retired. So the scheme worked out the pension you were due – so much percentage of your pay in say 1976 – and that was the same in cash terms when you retired, maybe 30 years later. In 1978, part of this pension (the bit that was in effect replacing your State Earnings Related Pension Scheme pension) had to be increased either by the rise in earnings or the rise in prices, though that could be capped at 5% a year. (In fact it was a bit more complicated than that but it's all history now and you are not going to be tested on it, so I'll leave it). Then from 1 January 1985 the rest of your preserved pension also had to be increased by the rise in prices, capped at 5% a year. At first that rule only related to the pension you earned from 1 January 1985. Then from the start of 1991 the pension you earned earlier also had to be increased by the same amount. These changes all applied to people who left their scheme after the change began. But some schemes decided to extend them to others as well, thus pushing themselves further into the mire of extra cost. And the more the pension scheme costs, the more someone has to put into it to make it balance. Turkeys voting for Christmas.

These were of course good changes for the individuals who left. They made things much fairer for them. But although it seems very unfair for someone who left after eight years paying into a pension to leave with nothing more than their contributions back and a tax bill, that was all part of the arithmetic of how pension funds worked. Stopping the unfairness has to be paid for by someone. The pension fund. And then of course if there isn't enough in it, the business that backs the scheme.

But from April 2005 there is a new change to reduce the costs to the fund. The rise of up to 5% a year has been cut to a maximum of 2.5% a year in order to limit the sums that the fund needs to set aside to meet these costs. It is the first erosion of the rights of pension-scheme members since, well, probably ever. And for collectors of TLAs, this whole business of increasing-a-pension-by-Inflation-but-no-more-than-a-certain-amount-which-was-5%-but-is-now-2.5% is called Limited Price Indexation, or LPI. Which is comfortingly similar to RPI – Retail Prices Index. But it is only the same as RPI if that is less than 5% – or 2.5% now. And just to confuse things further, LPI and how much it is also applies to the pension you are paid. But slightly differently.

BOSSES

The last bit was labelled 'politics' and it included a lot about bosses. This bit is called 'bosses' and has quite a lot of politics in it. Especially the Great Thatcherite Revolution of 1988 whose lasting legacy – pensions mis-selling and the loss of trust that resulted from it – is still with us. Another key feature of the dash for cash was removing the rule that allowed companies with good occupational pension schemes to make joining them compulsory (or, to use a more fashionable word at the time, a contractual obligation). That rule had the useful side-effect that because everyone had to join, no matter how short a time they secretly intended to stay, companies built in all those wonderful gains from early leavers. (I say 'secretly' in recognition of the fact that it is not a recommended technique to admit at your job interview that you are only joining the company to get a few lines on your CV before you bugger off.) But it also meant that everyone who worked for an employer with a pension scheme was in it.

> **DON'T WRITE**
>
> This box is here to prevent angry letters from women. I know that everyone in the company was not always also in the pension scheme. It was a sort of figure of speech. Many women were excluded from pension schemes, not on grounds of their sex but because they worked part time. Many schemes had a rule that said part-timers couldn't join the pension scheme. That of course discriminated most against women. Today there are 5.1 million part-time women and 1.2 million part-time men (and in the past the difference was larger) so any rule that penalises part-timers affects far more women than men. But it took many years before the courts ruled that was indirect sex discrimination and it was only from 1995 that pensions had to be made available equally to part-time workers. Like many other social advances, this one was entirely due to European law.

From 1 July 1988, companies could no longer make joining the scheme compulsory. So employees could have the freedom to give up a guaranteed pension that their boss mainly paid for, and choose instead to go for a pension that depended on the stock market doing well and to which their boss contributed nothing. That's what freedom of choice is all about. Or of course they didn't bother at all, neither joining their company scheme nor paying into one of their own, and relied – if they thought about it all – on the state.

The result is that more than a third of the people working for a company with a good pension scheme do not bother to join it.

Thanks Mrs T. But there is what our friends in computer programming call a work-around. It is called auto-enrolment (presumably because no-one could think of a TLA). And it means that although employers cannot make it compulsory to join their pension, they can make it automatic. In other words every new employee is automatically a member of the pension scheme unless they positively say 'No thanks'.

Around half the employers with salary-related schemes do that – mainly in the public sector – and around a quarter of those with money-purchase schemes. Automatic entry boosts the proportion joining from around two out of three to nine out of ten.

For several years the Government has considered making auto-enrolment compulsory. It knows the figures – indeed the Department for Work and Pensions gives even more dramatic figures than those above. Maybe it will get round to it one day. Perhaps before the crisis occurs. Especially as Lord Turner's Pension Commission now recommends it.

I've said it before and I don't want to have to say it again. Tidy your bedroom. And join your pension scheme if there is one. If you don't, you may find another unpleasant rule applies. If you don't join at once you may not be allowed to do so. Almost two out of three do not allow late entry, or make you beg if you ask for it. Others set a time limit. 'Well, if they can't decide to join within two years, that's it. I'm sorry.' And/or you may be too old to do so – some schemes say over 50 is too late. So join. Join now. And beg if you have to.

CONCLUSION

There is no one reason why pensions are in a mess. OK there may not be a crisis, yet. But no-one could say we'd got a Rolls Royce system that was set to glide effortlessly into the future. Increasing life expectancy has taken us by surprise. The reliance on shares as the main investment has been a mistake: it may have done well for a while, but it has hidden the cost and ignored the problems. And politicians and bosses have made it all much worse.

If pushed I would say the cause of the pension problems we all face can be summed up in four words. **We are living longer**. Then, if there's room, you could add three more **and no-one noticed**. And if you were being really unkind you could add **not least the actuaries**. You know, the people who make financial sense of the future.

CHAPTER FOUR

State Supremacy: Will the State provide?

Most people think the state pension is a joke. Often because their Gran lives on it and has no money, or their uncle lives off his investments and says the state pension is just enough to pay his weekly bill for gin and tonic. But actually the state pension can be good. Indeed it can be enough. And remember for a big chunk of the population, it *has* to be enough. They don't have anything else. And if you don't save save save, nor will you. I said earlier only three people understand the full (and exigent) details of the state pension. They all work for the Department for Work and Pensions and one of them thinks he might not be sure of all of it. Trouble is they don't work in the call centres and they didn't write the leaflet that explains it. By the end of this chapter, you will be the fourth. If you concentrate.

People write off the state pension because they hear it is £60 or £70 a week and they think, 'I couldn't live on that. Where would my second meal out come from?' The truth is the state retirement pension is actually £84.25 a week (cries of 'big deal') or £4,381 a year (louder cries of 'rubbish!'). Yes, I know it's not very much but that's only half the story – slightly less than half the story actually. But before we move on to the better bit, just think what £4,381 a year actually means – apart from what you probably spend down the pub. In a month. How much would you need in your pension pot to get a guaranteed pension that big, linked to price inflation, for life, at 65? If this were a TV programme I would now do what they call a reveal. The question would appear:

How big a pension pot
would you need to get
£4,381 a year for life
protected against inflation?

And then you would all write down 20 or 30 grand and we would wipe to reveal:

£90,725

Yep. You would need to save up £90,725 in your pension pot to have a pension equal to state retirement pension when you retire. And there is worse news. If you are a woman the figure is even higher. Pause. Wipe to reveal:

£100,500

That, of course, is because women live longer than men, so a pension for the rest of their life at 65 costs them more. And if you are what we might politely call an older woman (i.e. my age) and were born before 6 April 1950, then you can still draw your state pension at 60 rather than 65 – and to buy yourself a pension of £4,831 a year protected against inflation at the age of 60 you would need . . . longer pause, drum roll, reveal:

£115,100

Because not only do you live longer, but you get an extra five years at the start.

So although the state pension is not very much – and indeed is far too little to live on – you still need to save a hell of a lot to double it. And in that sense, that is what the state pension is worth – say in round terms £90,000 to a man and £100,000 to a woman. In fact it is worth even more than that because it brings with it benefits for widows and for partners who don't have a pension of their own. Adding those extra bits on would bring the total cost of replacing it in the market to well over £100,000. So before you sniff at the state pension remember what it is worth.

> In 1992 I wrote that the state pension – which was then £54 a week – was too little to live on. I got a letter from 64-year-old Nicola Hale who said 'nonsense young man' (which I wasn't really even then – young that is, not talking nonsense which I have made a career of for 20 years). 'I've lived on it for four years. I eat well, dress well and have plenty of holidays.' So I went to spend the day with her, found stylish clothes in charity shops, bought two pounds of carrots and potatoes in the market, spent £1 on five loo rolls and watched her haggle for 40p worth of bananas. At the end of the day, having studied her household bills, I was convinced she did it. But she is definitely the exception.

Fortunately the state pension doesn't end at £84.25 a week. Some people get almost three times that. How they do it we'll look at later, but first the basics of the state pension.

STOP!

Before you read about how the state pension works and why it is so little (yes, it is too little but is worth more than you think), there has been a lot of discussion about replacing it with something bigger and a lot simpler. Actually if the replacement required a claim in Mandarin Chinese and was calculated using differential calculus, it would be simpler. But the plans are to make it really really easy. Like, 'Hi, what's your name? Date of birth? Where do you live? How long? Good, here's £114 a week.' That plan for what is called a Citizen's Pension – paid to everyone just because they live here and have done for say ten of the last 20 years – may not happen. But an interesting compromise between that and the present system was put forward by Lord Turner in his second report at the end of 2005. He suggested that in future, as long as you are in the UK, that will count as a year's service towards a state pension. In other words, you will not have to pay National Insurance contributions (or have credits for them) for a year to 'count' towards your state pension. This controversial proposal may happen. Sometime. Certainly lots can change in the [fill in the gap] years before you reach 65. And the bigger the number you just wrote down, the more chance that something dramatic will happen.

But I don't have crystal balls, not even one, so all I can do is explain how the system works now. And once you understand it, well hey you might be able to get a job with the Department for Work and Pensions – and its staff get really good pensions. Problem solved!

Now you don't get the Basic State Pension just by being here (though the proposals above would eventually turn it into what is called a citizen's pension paid on exactly that basis, but they may never happen). No, you have to work for it. Roughly speaking you have to work for about 40 years to get the full £84.25 a week. Actually it is not working as such that counts, it is paying National Insurance contributions. Everyone in work earning over a certain amount pays those. Some people get them 'credited' – in other words although they have not actually paid contributions, the DWP will pretend they have when it does the sums. You get credits:

★ for the tax year you reach 16 and the next two tax years (Class 3 starting credits)
★ for the tax year you reach 60 and the next four years (these are called 'autocredits')
★ for a tax year in which you do 'approved training'
★ for weeks you get statutory maternity pay or statutory sick pay
★ for weeks you get jobseekers allowance
★ for weeks you get carer's allowance
★ for weeks you do jury service (but not if you are self-employed)
★ for weeks you get working tax credit
★ for weeks you were wrongly imprisoned

If you skipped that list or nodded off a bit while you read it, don't worry. I put it in (and you won't find it anywhere else outside official documents) just to show how stupid and complex all this is. But the credits for the first three years and the last five years of your working life are really useful. Add to that the fact that you can normally have five years without contributions and still get a full pension, and you can see that you can in fact doss around for a total of 13 years and still get a full pension at 65. So you can stay on at school, take a gap year, go to university, spend a year thinking what to do but not bothering to sign on as unemployed, leave work at 60 and still get a full pension. So although the amount is not very generous, the rules about getting it all are – quite.

WOMEN

The rules about qualifying for the state pension are generous but are also very much geared towards people who do have a fairly full working life, don't earn low wages and don't take pesky breaks to have children or look after Gran. Yep, designed by men for men. Which is why less than one in three women retiring today will get a full state pension. On average they have 70% of the full pension. Women under 40 are in a better position and the Government Actuary (him again) estimates that they will retire with as good (or bad) state pension entitlement as men.

If you do not plan things right though and you end up with fewer than the required years contributions (or credits), then you only get so many 44ths of your pension. So if you have a total of 40 years, you will get 40/44 or 91% of your pension (all these fractions are generously rounded up. OK, it's not so generous to round up 40/44 from 90.9 to 91, but if you had 26 years that is actually 59.1 and that is rounded up to 60. Don't say they don't look after you). If you are a woman born before 6 April 1960 then your pension age is less than 65 and your working life is less than 49 years (49 minus the five you are let off = 44 and that is used in the calculation). For an older woman it can be as little as 39 years and so the percentages are a bit different because they have 39 (or 40, 41, 42 or 43 depending when they were born) at the bottom of the fraction.

Women have a further complication – but hey they have better brains so they can cope with it. There is another way they can be helped to get 'enough' contributions for a full pension. Most women – and of course some men – spend quite a bit of their adult lives bringing up children. So they don't do paid work and don't pay National Insurance contributions for quite a long time. That leaves a gap in their National Insurance contribution record. The easy thing would be to give them credits to fill it. Is bringing up kids less important than jury service? Or going to university? Or being 60? I don't think so. But that would make life too easy. Now. Fractions. If the only thing you remember about fractions and percentages is tittering when you were told the sort that weren't percentages were called vulgar fractions then this next paragraph is going to get a bit tough.

Instead of giving women credits for each year they brought up children – in other words recognising that it may not be paid but it is bloody hard work and they deserve a credit for it – each year they spend bringing up kids is a year off their working life. Suppose a woman has three kids one after the other and spends 12 years out of the job market, returning when the final baby reaches three, those 12 years are taken off her working life. So instead of 44 (or those other numbers) it will be 32. If she then manages to accrue 32 years of contributions, she will get a full pension. If she only manages 22 instead of 22/44 or half the full pension, she will get 22/32 = (remembering to round up) 69%. At current rates that will give her an extra £832 a year in retirement, just for bringing up three kids for 12 years! Which, if you've ever done that job, may not seem all that generous. If she had got credits for those 12 years instead, she would have ended up with 34/44ths of her pension which is 78%, which would at least give her £1,226 a year in recognition of those 12 years bringing up children. But because it's done the way it is, it fulfils two key objectives of the state pension system: it is harder to understand and it gives women less. But at least today's mothers are better off than their mums. Even this half-generous rule did not apply for any years spent bringing up children before April 1978. This book is not a full guide to the state pension. But remember that to get this 'home responsibilities protection' as it is called, the mother must be the one to get the child benefit. If the child benefit is paid for some reason to the father, she will get nothing.

CARERS

Six million people in the UK devote their time to caring for a frail, sick or disabled relative or friend. Half of them also hold down a full-time job. Carers are estimated to save the country £57 billion a year – almost as much as the National Health Service costs. But half of them cannot do paid work as well – no wonder if you think about it – and some can get some small help from the state. Carer's Allowance is just £46.95 a week. To qualify a person must give at least 35 hours' care a week to someone who gets attendance allowance or the highest or middle rate of disability living allowance. The Carer's Allowance is taken away if they do paid work and earn £82 a week or more. People under 60 who get Carer's Allowance will normally get National Insurance credits. But if they cannot claim Carer's Allowance they will get Home Responsibilities Protection for each whole tax year they spend at least 35 hours a week looking after someone. But to get that they must register each year with the Department for Work and Pensions (well worth doing to help boost that state pension). And it will also help them boost their State Second Pension (which is explained below and it's more interesting than you might think). For the time they are caring they get credited for the State Second Pension as if they earned £12,500 a year for each year they get Carer's Allowance or Home Responsibilities Protection.

So, there are a lot of hoops to jump through and some complicated sums to calculate to get even the full Basic State Pension. Two final points to make. First, when you have paid enough to get the full pension, you might think you could stop paying National Insurance contributions. But no. They have to be paid until your 65th birthday (60th currently for women). And however much you pay above what is needed to get the full pension, you will never get more than 100% of it. Second, if the fraction works out that you will get less than 25% then you are in fact paid nothing. In some circumstances you can pay extra contributions to make up your record. It is often not worth it, but it can be if paying extra will bring you up from less than 25% where you get nothing to more than 25% where at least you get something.

ADDITIONAL PENSION

Now, about 2,000 words ago I said that the state pension could be boosted by almost twice as much again. And we are heading here for scandal territory – mis-selling of crap financial products on a massive and profitable scale. So even if you find the arithmetic a bit dull, you will love the tales of derring-do. Since 1978 when the woman I always call the Blessed Barbara was Secretary of State in charge of pensions, there has been an extra state pension called State Earnings Related Pension Scheme (SERPS) and, since April 2001, State Second Pension (and in fact officially throughout all that time simply 'additional pension'). It began life trying to give to people who had no company pension an extra state pension to match the best in the private sector. It never worked out like that but the additional pension is very worthwhile, despite being cut in half and in half again by the last Conservative government and changed again by the present Labour lot.

It is simply an earnings-related top-up to the state pension, and for people on not much more than average earnings it can boost the state pension by up to £146 a week. Remember the state pension is just over £84 a week, so the full SERPS of £146 on top nearly trebles it to a total of around £230 a week. And yes, that nearly trebles what a pension like that is worth. To buy an index-linked pension of £11,950 a year at 65 would cost a man aged 65 £247,000 and a woman £271,000. So the full state pension plus the full SERPS is a very worthwhile pension and far better than most people could ever achieve by saving up themselves. Sadly, most people do not have a large SERPS entitlement. Recently retired men have an average of just under £21 a week and recently retired women have well under half that – barely £9 a week. You might think that is because SERPS is earnings related and these people don't earn very much. Well, that plays a role. But the main reason is that the Government and the insurance industry conned them out of staying in SERPS.

SERPS is an arse-about-face kind of pension. Both SERPS and the Basic State Pension are paid for through National Insurance contributions. They cost people 11% of their earnings between £97 and £645 a week:

1% of that is for the NHS and the remaining 10% funds pensions and a few other benefits such as widow's benefits and maternity allowance. Everyone has the choice of opting out of SERPS and paying instead into a personal pension or a pension through their job. If they do that, their contributions are cut by 1.6% and they pay 8.4%. So 8.4% of your wages pays for a pension that is at the most £84.25 a week. And 1.6% of your wages pays for an extra pension that can be as high as £146 a week? This has come about through a fatal mixture of politics and arithmetic (they make chalk and cheese look the best of buddies). So the 1.6% of your pay that goes into SERPS looks like the pension bargain of the century. That worried the Tory government in the 1980s. Taxpayers of the future would simply not be able to afford it. They decided to tackle the problem.

First, SERPS was cut in half and then cut in half again. Few people noticed – it wouldn't happen for many years and it all seemed terribly technical. Then the Tories decided to slash the number of people who were in SERPS. At the time the only people who could opt out of SERPS already paid into a good company pension that would give them a guarantee of at least as much as SERPS, and in practice a lot more. That rule went so that anyone could opt out, as long as they paid into a pension of some sort. And then came the clever bit. A new sort of personal pension was invented that anyone could pay into. And if you opted out of SERPS into one of those, then the government would top up your contributions with all sorts of goodies. First the amount that SERPS would actually cost you was handed over and all the contributions that your employer would pay too. Then all the tax relief that you would get if your state contributions were paid in the private sector. Finally another percentage – a sweetener – was paid, taking the total amount for opting out of SERPS up from the 1.6% to something more like 8% of your pay. And it all came out of the National Insurance fund, which was in effect being raided to promote private pensions. There were adverts on the telly inviting people to 'set themselves free of their chains' (i.e. the state) and pay into their own little pot that no-one could take away.

Alas, the Government of the day had not taken account of the ingenuity of the financial services industry and the vicissitudes of the stock market. The latest estimates suggest that people who opted out of SERPS paid in £35 billion, of which the financial services industry creamed off around £3 billion, and the pension they get will be about a fifth lower than if they had stayed in SERPS all along. It is heading to be the sixth major mis-selling scandal since financial services were let loose on the general population in 1988.

The result is that although the maximum additional pension that can be paid is £146.12 a week, the average among those who retired in March 2005 was just £13.33 a week. And that consisted of an average of £20.96 among the men and £8.94 a week among the women. So Mrs T's policy worked. Additional pension is not a big drain on the National Insurance fund.

But if there is one piece of undoubtedly good pensions advice it is this – pay into the State Second Pension. If you have opted out, opt back in tomorrow, unless there's still time to do it today. You can only opt back in for whole tax years, but once the change is made it is backdated for the whole tax year. So as long as you do it by the last day of the tax year – 5th April – that counts for the whole tax year. If you want to put extra in your personal pension to make up what you have taken out to put into S2P, fine. It is probably a good idea. Belt and braces. Eggs in two separate baskets. So there will be something left for breakfast whatever happens. I wish I could follow my own advice. But I am self-employed and despite paying a hefty earnings-related National Insurance contribution, the self-employed only get the flat-rate Basic State Pension. We cannot join the State Second Pension.

> ## WOMEN
> It is usually women who are carers or who bring up children. They can get credited into State Second Pension as if they had earnings of £12,500 for each year they get Child Benefit for a child under 6 or Carer's Allowance or Home Responsibilities Protection as a carer.

There are others who cannot opt in either. They are:

- ★ **anyone in a company pension scheme that pays a pension related to their salary is automatically opted out of SERPS. Don't worry, your pension will be loads better.**
- ★ **some people in a company money-purchase scheme where the trustees have decided to save money by opting everyone out of SERPS. In this case, only the trustees can decide to let you opt back in. Lobby them.**

But anyone else who is an employee and earns at least £84 a week can and should be opted into State Second Pension.

Hang on a minute. The 1979–1997 government slashed SERPS in half twice, so it is worth now a quarter of what it might have been. The present Labour lot have threatened to turn it into a flat-rate pension. What faith can anyone have that it won't end up as money down the drain?

There are two answers to this, or maybe three. First, the future is not certain. But in the past when SERPS has been slashed, contributions paid so far have been honoured (at this point some older widowed women will leap forward and say that is not true and, to a very limited extent, they are right. But that was SERPS for widows, not the main SERPS). So at the moment SERPS contributions are a Good Thing. Second, if a government promise is uncertain, what then is a promise made by an investment linked to the stock exchange which siphons off at least 1.5% a year from the money you have saved whether it goes up or down? And third (I said there might be three), that is exactly the sort of argument used to mis-sell opting out of SERPS in the past and look where that got us.

> **Rule of Prosperity**
>
> **If you are contracted out of the State Second Pension contract back in.**

So trust me. I'm not a salesman. Opt back into S2P. One day you'll be glad you read this book.

PENSION CREDIT

I said earlier, and despite the Nicola Hale evidence, that the Basic State Pension was not enough to live on. And the Government agrees. No-one in the UK is expected to live on just the state pension. If they do then their income is topped up by Pension Credit to £114.05 a week. That is the level which the Government believes people aged 60 or more need to live on. And if their income is less than that, the Government will top it up until it reaches that amount. Someone on the Basic State Pension of £84.25 a week will get £29.80 a week more. Someone with a reduced state pension of say £58.13 a week because of missing contributions will get another £55.92. And someone who has no pension at all will be given, tax free and gratis, £114.05. So what is the point of the National Insurance system? What are all those complicated rules for? Because if you fail them you will get given a bigger pension anyway!

Welcome to the complicated, controversial and completely baffling world of means-tested benefits. The means test – an assessment of your 'means' including income and savings – is a much hated feature of the British system of social security (except by politicians, who love it – they call it targeting. Or in their more orotund mode, 'targeting the taxpayers' limited resources on those who need them most'). But for the people who have to fill in the form, reveal all their financial details (and it is not revealing their income they mind so much as telling someone about all their savings) and feel they are being patronised, means testing does not work. That is why around one and half million people over 60 who could get an average £15 a week each still do not claim the Pension Credit they are entitled to.

On the other hand there are loads of people who do not have an income of £114 a week who cannot claim. Couples, for example, are not entitled to £114 each – they have their joint income topped up to £174.05 between them. So a woman who has not paid enough National Insurance contributions to get a full state pension and who is married – or lives with someone as if they are married – cannot get her income topped up at all. Only if she and her partner between them have less than £174.05 a week can they get any extra. Savings count in a strange way too. Up to £6,000 (between you, if you are a couple) is ignored. The rest is converted into an income using tables that bear no relation to what the money actually earns.

Now you will be thinking, 'Hang on a minute, if I work hard and pay into the Basic State Pension I will get my £84.25 a week. Then if I pay into a personal pension as well, the first £29.80 a week I get is wasted because the Government would make that up anyway'. That was true. But it isn't now. At the expense of making Pension Credit even more complex, the Government introduced a new idea for those aged 65 or more only. Instead of losing their Pension Credit pound for pound they can keep a bit of it, in fact 60p in the pound. The result is that someone aged 65 who has a state retirement pension of £84.25 and a pension they have paid for of their own – or SERPS come to that – of £29.80 will get £17.88 in Pension Credit – it's called savings credit. And if you work that out it is 60% of the £29.80 they have worked for themselves. It is all mind-numbingly complicated but the result is that a single person with an income of £158.73 or less can get some Pension Credit – OK at that level it would only be 1p a week, but there it is.

The problem with means testing on this scale is that most of today's workers can look forward to a retirement when they depend on means-tested benefits. So the value of anything they save is reduced – even if they had not saved, they would get some if not all of the amount they have saved themselves. That makes it hard to be sure if saving is worthwhile and, if it is, how worthwhile. And that leads us to ask the people who sell us long-term investments, 'How can you be sure that the advice you give us is good?' We will return to this point again.

Before we leave means testing – stop groaning, this is important – it does not stop at Pension Credit. There is also help with, for example, council tax and rent. A single person with an income up to almost £200 a week who pays average council tax can get a discount off it. All these bits of means-tested help affect the value of saving. But the effect they have is too complex to work out or take account of when savings products are sold to us. And financial advisers, many of whom struggle to understand or explain things in their own bit of the world like risk or growth, cannot be expected to understand the state system.

PENSIONS FROM ABROAD

One final brief thought on state pensions. In this crazy international, jet-setting world we live in, more and more people will have worked in countries outside the UK. Most of these will have their own state pension system and most of them will allow you to claim that wherever you live in the world. So if you have worked in the USA or Europe, particularly for more than a year or so, it is worth checking whether you also have an entitlement to a pension from that country.

CHAPTER FIVE

Pensions at Work: Making your boss fork out

HOW THEY WORK

Pensions are often seen as a sort of deferred pay. In other words you are paid less now, the money is saved up and when you retire you are paid the money that was held back while you were working. And as it has been invested for many years, it will be rather more than the money you gave up. In a way your employer is taking responsibility for your whole life, not just the time you work there. In that sense pensions are an old-fashioned and paternalistic way of rewarding staff. Recent evidence shows that employers do not boast much about their pension scheme in job adverts and that could be because most workers do not really seem to value them. In fact, a significant proportion of people going into a job that offers a good pension scheme do not even bother to join it. That is foolish. In fact it is very stupid. Because the best kind of pension is one from your employer that they pay into as well as you.

Needless to say, employer's pensions come in a variety of types ranging from the gold plated to the black plastic sack. But the key thing is that the employer pays into the scheme. So part of the money you live off in retirement comes from your employer not from you. In some cases it all comes from the employer. And of course some of it will come from the Chancellor – which really means other taxpayers – through the tax relief you get on the money you pay into a pension.

Pensions from work have had a bad press over the last couple of years, with pension schemes closing down and people who thought they had been promised a pension finding out that the fund had too little money and that they could expect only a fraction of the pension they had been promised. Those stories are true and the hardship severe. But they are very very rare. Not joining a scheme because of these problems is like not going out because 11 people a day die on the roads. More on this later.

Here is a quick guide to what your employer may offer you:

★ **Salary-related schemes** – promise you a pension which is a certain percentage of your salary. Nowadays these schemes are often called 'defined benefit' schemes because the amount of the pension, the benefit, is guaranteed or defined. And also because it is harder to understand. Join it.

★ **Money-purchase schemes** – save up all the contributions made by you and your employer into your own pension fund, which is invested. Your pension is whatever you can buy with that fund when you retire. Nowadays they are normally called 'defined contribution' schemes because it is the amount you pay in which is fixed, not the pension you get at the end. And see above re harder to understand. Join it and pay in the amount needed to maximise the contribution your employer pays in.

★ **Stakeholder schemes** – some employers will offer a stakeholder scheme instead of either a salary-related or a money-purchase scheme. There is nothing wrong with stakeholders. They are just another kind of money-purchase scheme. But normally it means that the employer does not put any money into it. So all the contributions going in are yours. Better to choose your own pension arrangements.

★ **AVCs** – the letters stand for additional voluntary contributions. They are a way to top up your employer's scheme. Occasionally the employer will put in some contributions too. Normally they will not. But it may still be better to use the scheme your employer offers.

★ **Salary sacrifice** – this is not a kind of pension but a way of paying for it. You agree to a pay cut. That saves you and your employer the National Insurance contributions on your pay. The extra can be used to boost the contributions into a pension. Can be a good idea, mainly for employers. Make sure you share in the savings.

End of the instant guide, which would get you through a round of *Who Wants to Be a Millionaire* if you were ever asked a question about money. The details follow.

SALARY-RELATED SCHEMES: THE GOLD STANDARD

A pension that is guaranteed to be a proportion of your pay for the rest of your life is the gold standard. If your employer offers one and you do not join it, then you should be sacked for incompetence.

> ### Rule of Prosperity
>
> **If your company has a salary-related pension scheme, join it.**

Not all salary-related schemes are the same. But basically they work like this. Each year you belong to the scheme you earn a pension which is a fraction of your pay. The most common fraction is 1/60th. Now that may not sound much, and for one or two years' work it is not. But if you work there ten years you get a sixth, after 20 years it is a third and so on. And if you work there all your working life, say 40 years, you get 40/60ths which is two thirds of your pay as a pension. Some are less generous and you earn 80ths of your pay. A few are more generous, such as the very liberal scheme offered to MPs which pays 40ths. In the past there was a limit which meant that the pension paid could never be more than two thirds of your salary. But that legal limit has now been scrapped, although most pension schemes retain it in their own rules. In future those rules could be changed to allow MPs, for example, to have a pension after 40 years which equalled their salary of around £60,000 a year.

The scheme may also offer life insurance, a pension for your widow or widower and inflation proofing of up to 5% a year for the pension itself. You can also cash in some of the pension to get a tax-free lump sum. In the past if you got two thirds of your pay as a pension and you took the maximum lump sum, then 3/80ths of your pay for each year of membership, that was reckoned to be about the same as earning 80ths. These limits have been changed from A-Day and schemes will be free if they want to change them.

At this point the more curious among you will have a number of questions. One is what do they mean by 'your pay'. In the past, they were called 'final salary' schemes and the pension was related to your pay in the last few years of your employment, usually the average or the best of the last three years. Hence the fashion for promoting senior people to well-paid sinecures just before they retired. It kept them out the way and kept them quiet by the promise of a great pension. For people in professional jobs, final salary schemes made sure that the pension reflected their highest pay. But recently some schemes have changed to base the pension on a figure representing the average pay you have earned during your whole time in the scheme. That reduces the cost in most cases, though for people in more manual work it may actually boost their pension as earnings tend to peak in their 40s, rather than their 50s or 60s. It also stops the scandal of giving people those well-paid sinecures at the end of their working lives (though some companies who make this change retain final salary schemes for directors and senior managers. I wonder why?)

If you keep your old wage slips (sad bastard) you will know that many years ago you were paid far far less than you are now. And not just through promotion but because wages rise each year as pay deals come through. Typically pay rises faster than inflation: currently it is rising by 4.2% a year, compared with inflation of 2.5% a year. At that rate pay will double over around 17 years. So a pension related to what you were paid many years ago is not much good. That is dealt with in the calculation by revaluing your pay each year, usually in line with the index of average earnings produced by the Government but it is up to the scheme to decide how it will revalue your earnings. It could for example revalue them in line with its own annual pay deals. So at the end of your 40 years or so there will be a record of each year's pay which will be re-valued in line with earnings (or whatever the scheme rules say), the average will be calculated and your pension will be so many 80ths of that. The same process is used even for final salary schemes. They sometimes take the best or the average pay you received out of the last three years before retirement. And again each year's pay for those years will be revalued in line with average earnings.

At least that is how it works if you stay in the job until you retire. If you leave the job before you retire, the same problem arises – but it is dealt with very differently. Suppose you worked for Whiz Kids Ltd for ten years from 1988. Then you might have earned £18,000 a year when you left in 1998, aged 35. When you reach 65 in 2028 you will be due a pension from Whiz Kids of 10/80ths or one eighth of the pay you earned when you were with them. One eighth of £18,000 is £2,250, which in another ten or so years would be worth very little indeed. If they revalued it in line with earnings of course it wouldn't matter. To date £18,000 increased at 4% a year – roughly the rate of wage inflation – would be worth £24,600. By the time you retire that would have reached more than £58,000 so you would get an eighth of that, which would be £7,250. Not a fortune but well worth having. Unfortunately that is not how it works. Between leaving the scheme and pension age your wages will be re-valued in line with the rise in prices, which is usually a lot less than the rise in wages and is capped at 5%, and 2.5% from April 2005. What it should mean is that whatever £1,500 would have bought in 1998 it will still buy the same amount in 2028. So it is fair in a way. But not as good as if you had stayed in the job and the scheme. If inflation over that time is 2.5% then your pension would be based on a 'salary' of £32,000 and would be worth £4,000. Those of you who are checking this with a calculator to hand will realise that all these figures are rounded drastically, but that is because estimates of this sort are subject to huge errors.

Fortunately if you leave a job, you do not have to leave your pension behind. You can move it to your new job. That may or may not be a good idea. See **Moving on** below.

WHO PAYS FOR IT?

Ah. Well. This is the problem. It can't have escaped your notice that promising to pay people a pension of a certain amount in the future is going to be expensive. Take that pension you are due from Whiz Kids. I worked out it would be £4,000 in 2028 when it was due. At current prices, it would cost about £90,000 to buy a guaranteed pension for life of £4,000 a year which rose each year with inflation. Over your ten years at Whiz Kids with promotions and so on you earned around £120,000 and you paid 5% of that into the pension scheme, which is £6,000. Your employer didn't pay a fixed amount into the scheme, but they have to guarantee that there will be enough to pay your pension and of course those due to everyone else. So they have to guarantee that there will be £90,000 with your name on it by 2028. Now you paid in £6,000. If that grows at 6% a year over the 30 years between your leaving Whiz Kids and retiring, it will be worth about £35,000. So your employer will have to put in about £10,000 and between you that £16,000 will grow to reach £90,000 in time for your retirement. That doesn't sound too bad does it? You put in 6%, your employer puts in 8.5% and bingo. That should be how things work. But you are a cheap employee. Remember you left early, so your pension is only £4,000. If you had stayed on it would be £7,250 – and to buy a pension of that size would cost more like £160,000. And your employee would have to put in more than £20,000 compared with your £6,000. Which would be about 17% of your pay. Now all this is very approximate. And no doubt any actuary reading this will be tut-tutting and saying, 'what about . . .' and 'he's forgotten . . . .' and 'it doesn't take account of . . . .'. Well all that is true. It is approximate (stifled laughter – unlike the predictions actuaries have made about pensions and life expectancy over the last 50 years). And that is the point. It is about the distant future. It assumes that inflation will be 2.5% a year and wage growth will be 4% a year and that the return on the pension fund investments will be 6% a year. It also assumes that the cost of buying a pension for life in 2028 will be the same as it is now. None of those may turn out to be correct. But using those figures, you can see that to pay a pension of half your pay after 40 years' contributions takes joint contributions from you and your employer of just over 17.5% of your pay. So if you pay 5%, your employer pays 12.5%. So if all those assumptions turn out to be right, then the fund will just have enough to pay up. And in fact that is just about how much is paid in. The latest figures from the National Association of Pension Funds show that employees pay 5% and employers 16%. A total of 21% of your pay saved up to pay you during the long holiday at the end of your life.

Trouble is, the fund doesn't have to have just enough if everything turns out as expected. It has to guarantee it even if everything turns out wrong. And just about all those figures could be wrong. Pension fund growth, the return on the investment, was rather more than 6% a year in the last quarter of the last century, but has been rather less in the first few years of this century. Growth of 6% a year – after charges and costs – is a fairly ambitious target, though widely used. Suppose it was 5% not 6%. Your pension would be almost a fifth less. Or rather your employer would have to pay in 16.7% instead of 12.5%. Suppose that the cost of buying you a pension at retirement doubled (and it has done that over the last 15 years). Well, your pension would halve – or rather your employer would have to put in 38% of your pay. And this is the real problem with salary-related schemes. They make promises – which is good. But they may not be able to keep them. Which is bad.

Of course these problems with salary-related schemes have always existed. But they have become much more apparent recently for a number of reasons.

★ **From the mid 1970s to 1999 the stock market went only one way – up. The price of shares grew on average by 12% a year, double the rate – before charges – assumed in the calculations above.**
★ **In the past, pension schemes got a big boost from early leavers. Anyone who left within the first five years of joining was given back their own contributions, but any investment growth those**

contributions had earned (and in some cases the contributions made by the employer) were kept by the fund for the benefit of members who did not leave. That no longer happens.
* Even when the pension was under-funded it was much easier in the past to hide the fact and hope that investment growth would pick up and cover the gap in the future. But new accounting standards – cryptically called FRS17 – now mean that the deficit of the pension scheme has be to be calculated each year and be placed in full view on the company accounts.

Because shares recently have been disappointing as investments, the money saved for our pensions has grown more slowly than was expected. It is the double whammy. The funds are smaller. And they have to stretch over more time. Inevitably they are thinner. Add changes to accountancy rules that make pension deficits much more obvious and expensive to shareholders, and the twin political problems of the past Government forcing companies to stop paying into schemes when they seemed too big (and many of them joining in with a vengeance) and then the present Government taking away tax relief on dividends earned by pension funds, and you have a looming pension crisis. Whatever the political answers, each one of us can do more to try to boost our own pension. We may not be able to retire at 50, but we can at least make sure we can retire at 65.

SCHEMES CLOSING

With all these uncertainties it is no wonder that companies are pulling back from the expense and uncertainty of salary-related pension schemes. The Mercer consulting company estimates that the biggest 350 companies in the UK have a total deficit on their pension schemes of £76 billion. And to reduce it they are boosting the amount paid into the schemes by 65%. Nevertheless, the same study said it will take 12 years to clear the pension deficits. So companies are pulling out. In 2003 a quarter of these schemes closed to new entrants. In other words, if you join the company now you will not be entitled to join the same pension scheme as those who are already there. That is bad news for those who want to follow the first Rule of Prosperity and join a salary-related scheme. But they do still exist, not least in places where the cost of the scheme is not an issue. Welcome to the magical world of the public sector.

Some of the best, and certainly the safest, salary-related pensions are found in the public sector. Civil servants in national and local government, teachers, doctors and nurses and their support staff, police officers, fire fighters and the armed forces all enjoy benefits which are generally better than the best pensions paid by companies. The schemes pay two thirds of their salary after 40 years (normally taken as half their pay plus a lump sum) and they can retire on full benefits at 60. Early retirement on full benefits on grounds of ill health is common and some of the schemes allow for normal retirement at 55.

Employees pay in to their scheme, usually slightly more than in the private sector. Most pay 6% of their pay and police officers and fire fighters pay 11%. But others pay a lot less. Civil servants pay 1.5% or 3.5% depending on the scheme they join and members of the armed forces pay nothing, though that may change.

Clearly contributions like that cannot pay for the benefits enjoyed by the contributors. Though when I wrote that some years ago in *Saga Magazine* an irate police officer wrote to me saying that 'I pay for my pension every month out of my pay and I am sick to death of you journalists claiming they are paid for by council tax payers'. I felt if he had actually met me I would have spent the night in the cells! But sadly he was wrong. Unlike normal pension schemes, in the public sector there is generally no 'fund' to make up the difference. Instead, the state simply pays the pensions out of taxation. And before local government workers write me abusive letters, their scheme is the one major exception. It is funded. But even in schemes that are funded – Members of Parliament, university teachers and staff, former British Coal workers, the BBC, Royal Mail, Bank of England, Civil Aviation Authority and London Transport – the state will ultimately make up any shortfall. In 2003/04 unfunded pensions cost taxpayers £18 billion – in other words if we did not have to pay these pensions we could just about scrap council tax. Or slash the basic rate of tax from 22p in the pound to 16p. Or cut VAT from 17.5% to 13.5%. So it is a lot of money.

> **Rule of Prosperity**
>
> **If you want a good and secure pension, get a job in the public sector (and join the pension scheme!) .**

You might at this point ask yourself, 'if we can afford these decent pensions for workers in the public sector, why can't we afford them for everyone in work?' In other words, pay everyone a pension of two thirds of their pay in work. It is an excellent question. The Blessed Barbara Castle tried to do just that with her SERPS, which was supposed to offer to everyone a pension as good as the best in the private sector. But politicians in all parties baulked at the cost. So the only answer to that sensible question is that it would cost too much. There are about five million people in these public sector schemes, out of 29 million people in work altogether. So if paying these pensions to 5 million public employees costs £18 billion, paying something similar to everyone would cost almost six times as much – around another £90 billion. Which would put up income tax by 20p in the pound. Or more than double VAT to 38%.

Of course it is not that simple. But it would be very expensive and that is why civil servants and MPs, who have these pensions, say we could not possibly afford them for everyone else. Hmmm.

Of course in some countries such pensions are paid to everyone, or nearly. And I don't mean in La La Land or over the rainbow. You only have to go a few kilometres from the UK to find much better pensions. Because in fact state pensions paid in the UK are just about the worst in Europe. Go to France, Germany, Italy, even the Czech Republic, and you will find that the state pension is (a) related to your earnings and (b) higher, usually much higher, than the pension paid here. Now I know the grass is always greener on the other side of the Channel, but it is true. Of course they pay for these pensions. The money doesn't come from a Euro machine in the sky. Taxes are higher. In Germany, for example, people take home less than half the headline salaries they are paid. And a lot of these schemes are in trouble for the same reason that pensions everywhere are in trouble: we are living longer. Sorry I'll say that again. WE ARE LIVING LONGER. Some countries are therefore considering raising the state pension age. So we could have better state pensions. We would just have to pay higher taxes. Or rather, for you to have a better state pension, your children and grandchildren would have to pay higher taxes. And they might not want to.

It is not only the amount of pension paid in public sector schemes which is better than typical pensions in the private sector. They are also more certain to be paid. Ultimately the state will pay up – which means taxpayers, you and me. Whereas in the private sector the promise made is only as good as the company that makes it.

ARE THEY SAFE?

If you have read anything about pensions in the press in the last few years, you will know that some salary-related pension schemes are in trouble. An estimated 85,000 people have been told they will not be paid the pension they were promised. And no less than two rescue schemes have been set up by the Government. Before we look at them, why are they needed? If you cast your mind back to 5 November 1991, as people in the UK prepared to celebrate Guy Fawkes night, the overweight newspaper magnate Robert Maxwell slipped naked from the Lady Ghislaine (his yacht) into the sea off the Canary Islands. His body was found a few hours later. Within weeks it emerged that the man *Private Eye* had always called 'the bouncing Czech' had stolen £480 million from the Mirror Group pension fund to help prop up his failing business empire, which had £3 billion of debts. Questions were asked. Enquiries were set in train. A rescue fund was started. And the rules for pension funds were tightened up. No more could they be used as a piggy bank by the company which sponsored them. The powers of trustees were strengthened. And something comfortingly called the 'minimum funding requirement' was invented. All pension funds had to meet this minimum funding requirement, and you may think it was the minimum amount of money they needed to meet their pension promises. Many people did. Alas it was not. It was hedged round with get-out clauses allowing schemes to put off meeting it for years. And even when they did, it was only enough as long as the pension fund carried on taking in contributions from existing members and attracting new ones. If it closed, if contributions stopped and new members did not replace the ones that retired, then the MFR was sadly inadequate. As long as the company that promises the pensions is trading and solvent, that does not really matter. It has a duty to pay sufficient into the fund to make sure the promises are kept. And recently many large companies have paid very large sums into their funds for that purpose.

So the sad inadequacy of the MFR became apparent slowly. The changes themselves had only come into force in April 1997, more than seven years after the Mediterranean splash made by Robert Maxwell washed over pension schemes in London. Such is the rapidity of action shown by lawmakers whose own pension scheme is loftily above such crimes. But as the 21st century began it was becoming obvious that some companies were either going bust or being taken over and leaving the pension fund with too little money to meet the promises made to the people who had worked there. When that happens the scheme has to go into a different mode. It is 'wound up' and the fund is used to buy annuities to continue the pensions of retired members and to provide pensions for those who will retire in future. The rules state that existing pensioners have the first call on this money and they normally continue to get their full pension. Those who have not retired then share out what is left, which is usually not enough to pay their pensions in full – sometimes hardly at all.

After a long period of denying there was any problem, then saying it could not possibly estimate the extent of it, and whatever it was the problem was someone else's responsibility, the Government was finally forced to admit that up to 40,000 people could expect half or less of the pension they had been promised and another 35,000 would probably get a pension between a fifth and half of what they expected. It then announced a rescue plan, the Financial Assistance Scheme (or FAS), which would give some help to some of these people. Hedged round with rules and restrictions, the scheme is expected to start paying out around April 2006 to people whose scheme got into trouble in the eight years between April 1997 and April 2005. The amounts paid out will be very small. The scheme will be expected to use the money it has to buy the best pension it can for the people not yet retired. FAS will then step in and top up that pension to 80% of what the person would have got if they had retired at the scheme pension age. But:

- ★ **There is nothing for younger people. Anyone who will reach the pension age of their scheme after 14 May 2007 will get nothing. So someone who reaches 58 in April 2006 will be too young.**
- ★ **Nothing will be paid until they reach 65, even if the scheme pension age was younger. Someone who was 57 on 14 May 2004 who expected to draw a scheme pension at 60 in May 2007 will now have to wait until they reach 65 on 14 May 2012.**
- ★ **The pension will not be increased each year with inflation. So over 20 years with inflation around 3% a year, its real value will halve.**
- ★ **There will be an upper limit of £12,000 on the total pension paid. This upper limit will not increase over time.**

Widows and widowers will get half the pension the member would have got.

So it is one small step in the right direction. But hardly a giant leap. The reason for mentioning it at all – and in some detail because it almost certainly will affect very few people reading this book – is to make clear that pensions are fraught with dangers. The pension schemes that people paid into were compulsory until 1988, and were recommended by the Government, and were said to be safe and even guaranteed right up to 2001. Despite that, the Government has produced very little except disappointment for this small minority of people.

PENSION PROTECTION

From April 2005 an entirely different sort of protection began. It is called the Pension Protection Fund or PPF and is supposed to end once and for all the danger of your pension all but disappearing if your scheme is wound up after your employer goes out of business.

If that happens, from April 2005 the scheme and all its assets should be taken over by the fund. Needless to say, there is a welter of new jargon and terms and not all schemes that go belly up (to use a technical term) after that date will be included. But almost all of them should be. The fund then pays out the promised pensions, or a proportion of them, up to certain limits. These are more generous than the Financial Assistance Scheme. If that was a small step, the Pension Protection Fund is a stride or two. But still not a giant leap.

People who have not yet retired when the fund takes over will get less pension than they were promised by the scheme.

The pension will be 90% of what they were promised at the scheme pension age, subject to an overall cap of £25,000. This pension will have very limited protection against inflation. As prices rise, the value of money becomes less. At the moment the inflation rate which is used to index pensions is just under 3% a year. And many schemes will pay up to 5% inflation on their pensions. But pensions taken over by the PPF will be limited to 2.5% a year, and that will only apply to the part of the pension earned from April 1997. Pension earned before that will not be inflation proofed at all. So someone who retires in 2007 after 40 years' service, with three quarters of their pension earned before 1997 and a quarter since, will see it raised by a quarter of 2.5% or 0.6% a year.

People who have already retired will normally get the pension they are already getting. But these will also be subject to the restricted inflation proofing. Someone already in their 70s may find the pension is never increased again with inflation.

People who have retired early, before the age laid down by the scheme, will be subject to the 90% and £25,000 cap. So these early retirers could find their pensions cut once the PPF takes them over.

There is a danger that even these limited pensions will be cut in the future. The cost of the PPF was originally estimated by the Government at around £300 million a year. But for 2006/07 the PPF has fixed it at £575 million and some actuaries estimate it could be double that in a few years. These costs are borne by the schemes that still exist and that ultimately means the big companies who run them. Within weeks of the PPF beginning, the Confederation of British Industry – which represents those big employers – began lobbying for the costs of the scheme to be controlled by a combination of a subsidy from taxpayers and reducing the pensions that are paid. The Government has made it clear there will be no subsidy from taxpayers. They say it would be unfair to do that as many of those taxpayers do not have access to a good pension scheme. So if the costs of the scheme grow substantially, the Government will come under pressure to reduce the pensions paid. The Government has not ruled that out, and it does have the power to make such cuts.

END OF SALARY-RELATED PENSIONS

The cost of the PPF is just one reason why many experts predict that the days of salary-related pension schemes – at least run by private companies – are numbered, and that the number is fairly small.

The essential problem with salary-related pension schemes is this. They make promises about the pension you will get. Now obviously that is also their tremendous strength – for you. But for the company and its board, and especially the Finance Director whose job is not to run the finances (that is an administrative task that can be out-sourced, and often is) but to save money, that is a serious hitch. And the promises made by salary-related schemes are very expensive and nowadays clearly shown on the accounts.

Just about all these schemes belong to the National Association of Pension Funds and its Chief Executive, Christine Farnish told Radio 4 in June 2005 that 'final salary schemes are history, frankly'. She returned to the theme in October, commenting on the rising costs saying, 'an inevitable consequence is that companies will be quietly getting out of final salary schemes'. Her fears were supported by experts at the Cass Business School Pensions Institute, who predicted in the same month that final salary pension schemes would all be closed with five years. Commenting on the PPF and other new obligations on pension funds Cass said, 'there is no point in having the best regulation in the world if there are no schemes left to regulate'.

It is not just regulation. Collectively the UK's final salary schemes need another £130 billion, on top of existing investments of £600 billion, to have enough money to meet their pension promises. These deficits now have to be explicitly stated in the company accounts, and that leads to nervousness among shareholders and pressure on directors to control them. One way of doing that is to close the scheme to new members. Already about three quarters of salary-related schemes have taken that step and every year more are following. When that happens, the scheme is still 'live' and people who have joined before that date carry on paying in. But no new members can join and as the existing members retire or die the assets of the scheme shrink. The next step after closing to new members is to stop further contributions from existing members. In other words, the salary-related pension is still promised for all service up to a certain date. But from then, no further service counts. Late in 2005, Rentokil became the first major company to take this step, though many smaller ones have quietly done so. The Cass Business School in London says most, if not all, schemes will follow by 2010.

The third stage is to wind up the scheme. That means using the assets to buy guaranteed pensions from insurance companies to meet the promises made and close the scheme. New laws which seek to guarantee the amount of pension that is bought make this quite an expensive option. But over the next 20 years or so, many experts fear it will happen to most schemes. In 2004 there were barely *half* the number of salary-related schemes that existed in 2000.

So if you want a salary-related pension that has a hope of survival, get a job in the public sector and join the pension scheme.

MONEY PURCHASE: DEBASED COINAGE

If your company does not offer a salary-related pension it will offer what is called a money-purchase scheme or, same thing, a 'defined contribution' scheme. Many employers offer both – salary-related for existing staff and money-purchase for new staff. And if salary-related schemes are closed to existing members too, in future they will have to pay in to a money-purchase scheme.

Both names – money purchase and defined contribution – are of course meaningless in any normal use of English. The two-word phrase 'money purchase' comes from the fact that the contributions paid in by you and your employer – the 'money' – is saved up in a little pot with your name on it. You see they're doing it again. As soon as you ask a simple question – what does money purchase mean – they resort to kiddy language. As if you are stupid. Or five. Or both. There is no pot. And it doesn't have your name on it. What there is in fact is a huge fund invested in various things. A computer keeps records of what you've paid in. And if you ever want it back when you retire or change jobs, it works out how much of it is yours depending on how much you have put in, how long each contribution has been there and how much it has grown.

OK. I'll talk about a little pot with your name on it, it's simpler. And when you retire you have to use the money in that pot to 'purchase' a pension. Hence 'money' 'purchase'. How big that pension is depends on how much the money in the pot is worth and general economic conditions when you retire. Longer life and lower interest rates mean smaller pensions. Guess which way life and interest rates are going now?

The alternative name – 'defined contribution' – was invented to distinguish these pensions from the salary-related schemes. In the latter it is the pay-out that is guaranteed – it is a proportion of your salary – so they are called 'defined benefit' schemes because the pay out or 'benefit' is 'defined'. So by way of contrast, money-purchase schemes are called, no not 'undefined benefit' – that would be too true and helpful, but 'defined contribution' schemes as it is the amount you pay in that is guaranteed by the scheme, rather than the amount it pays out by way of pension. Big deal.

Just to make the whole thing more esoteric and impenetrable, defined benefit schemes that pay a pension related to your salary are abbreviated to DB. And defined contribution schemes, which don't, are abbreviated to DC. These similar and obscure acronyms finally squeeze any meaning out of the terms. And have the further advantage that they are only understood by people who can then charge large amounts of money to sell them.

Enough of words, what about substance? Whichever sort of pension scheme you belong to, tax relief is given; both you and your employer pay in, and the money is invested in much the same way. So ultimately it shouldn't matter which of these two sorts of pension you have. If the same amount goes in and the investment is the same after 20 years they should be worth the same. Shouldn't they? Mmm. That conclusion sadly isn't even half true.

First, the companies which operate money-purchase pension schemes pay in far less than those which run salary-related schemes. The average paid into a money-purchase scheme by an employer is 7.6%. But for salary related schemes it is 16.1%. Members pay in about the same – a shade over 5%. So the big difference between the two is not so much the guarantees as the fact that only a little more than half as much (12.8% compared to 21.2%) goes into the money-purchase scheme. Given that most salary-related schemes promise a pension of half your pay, on average you might expect a shade over a quarter of your pay from the money-purchase scheme.

But you'd be wrong. There is another reason why these schemes pay out smaller pensions. Remember the £130 billion deficit? These schemes have total investments of £600 billion. But they are £130 billion short of the money needed to meet their promises. That is what the deficit means. So the money in salary-related pension funds should be over a fifth more than it is if they are to honour the pension promises they have made. So the money paid in, even though it is twice what is contributed to the money-purchase schemes, needs to be boosted by more than a fifth to pay a pension of half your salary. That implies that the money-purchase schemes on the funding they get will pay out around a fifth of your pay. Here's the sums:

£600 billion is 21.2% of pay. Add £130 billion to give £730 billion, and that will represent 25.8% of pay. That pays a pension of half pay. But only 12.1% goes in to money-purchase schemes. So they will pay 12.1/ 25.8 x a half (0.5) = 23.4%, between a fifth and a quarter. I know it's rough and ready. But it gives us a good guide.

The third reason why even this estimate is probably too high relates to the way the pensions are actually paid. With a salary-related scheme the money in the fund is actually used to pay the pension. With a money-purchase scheme the pension is bought from an insurance company. And they tend to be cautious, having got their fingers burned in the past, so will tend to pay out less for the same degree of funding than a pension fund would. One reason why the minimum funding requirement is not enough to pay the pension promised when a scheme is wound up is that buying an annuity to pay a pension is much more expensive than paying it yourself out of a scheme that is continuing. So if you expect your pension fund to provide a pension of around a sixth of your pay, you may be somewhere along the right track .

Surely though you will think this won't apply to those schemes which convert from salary related to money purchase. They want to control risk and administrative costs and the fees charged by the PPF. Not save money. Ha ha. Ho ho ho. Ha di bloody ha. No. Sadly, the evidence shows that the Finance Directors of these companies cannot resist the opportunity to change from a risky and expensive scheme and to make the replacement not just not risky but also much cheaper. They cut the company contribution into the scheme dramatically. Well, by around a half anyway, leaving new employees in a much worse scheme than their lucky colleagues who have been there longer. That's why I call them debased coinage rather than the gold standard of salary-related schemes.

But despite these problems, the next rule of prosperity is:

> ## Rule of Prosperity
>
> **If your company has a money-purchase pension which it pays into, join it.**

That's because although the contributions into a money-purchase scheme are less than those into a salary-related scheme, they do still exist. One estimate suggests that more than 3.5 million employees could join a company pension scheme but don't bother. They are all giving up a pay rise, worth about £5 billion a year between them. It's plain daft.

Whatever the pension fund is worth, and it will always be less than you hoped, you can take a quarter of it as a tax-free lump sum if you want and the rest has to be used to buy a pension for life – what is normally called an annuity. So the pension you get will depend on two things, or so:

1. The size of the fund. And that will depend on:
   a. how much has been paid in and
   b. how much that has grown, which of course depends on
      i investment performance and
      ii. how long it has been there
2. The annuity you can buy. And that will depend on:
   a. interest rates, which depend on
      i. when you retire
      ii. the economic circumstances then
   b. predictions of longevity, which depend on
      i. your age
      ii. your sex
      iii. your health
      iv. if you are married
   c. whether you want it
      i. fixed

    ii. rising each year
        1. with inflation
        2. at 3%
  d. who you buy it from

Well, that's 20 variables. To say the pension you get is 'uncertain' is a bit like saying Elton John likes flowers. There is a whole subchapter on the choices you face later because it has more general application than this. But you can see the problem. Paying into a money-purchase pension is a pig in a poke. You pay your money. But until you retire and are allowed to open the sack, you will never know if you have a plump sow that can breed and feed you for 20 years or a scrawny porker that will give you a couple of rashers of salt bacon a month.

OTHER PENSIONS

You will be told there are loads of other sorts of pension – and you will have acronyms shoved down your throat until you bring up alphabet spaghetti. But that is just done to bamboozle you. And while you are bent over the white basin someone will be emptying your pocket. Trust me: there are two sorts of pension, and that's it. Either your employer promises to pay you a pension of a size related to what you earned. Or you have your own pension pot and you have to buy a pension with it. Everything else is a variation on these two things – in fact almost always a variation on the latter. Bear that in mind. It will help with the acronyms.

TOP-UPS

However good your scheme, you might want to put more into a pension than the few percent you and your boss put in between you. It can be a good idea. But you have to know first what sort of scheme you are in now, and then decide what sort you want to go in. So we're back to the big division between salary related and money purchase.

If you are in a **salary-related** scheme, the pension you are promised is bigger the more years you have paid in. You get 1/60th or 1/80th or some such of your pay for each year of membership. Some schemes – fewer and fewer but they still exist – allow you to buy what are called added years. In other words you pay in more money either as a lump sum or extra monthly contributions. And the scheme counts you as if you have been there for an extra year, or more if you pay more. There will be a limit to how many added years you can buy, but they are always the best option if they are available. Ask the person who runs your scheme about them.

If added years are not available or if you are in a **money-purchase** scheme, you can still pay more into a pension. The limits for how much you can put in are so generous (you and your employer between you can put in your whole year's pay up to a limit of £215,000) that for most people they can put in as much as they can afford. There are two ways to do this – though more and more they are becoming one way.

The traditional way was to put money into what was catchily called Additional Voluntary Contributions, better known as AVCs (so I will use the TLA here as it is almost a word in itself, like a PIN. Except that AVC is pronounced the same as it is spelt A-V-C.). Every company scheme offered AVCs and in most cases you could pay in directly out of your pay. That made it easy and, because the company had arranged the AVCs, the charges were usually fairly low. They were called 'in-house AVCs' and most companies would even offer you a choice between two or three in-house AVC providers. Choosing between them was normally impossible to do rationally but (a) It gave you the illusion of some sort of freedom and (b) meant that If the one you chose did really badly, the employer could (elbows into waist, hands upturned, mouth in a turned-down smile) honestly say 'nothing to do with me, guv'.

The alternative was to buy AVCs on your own, separately from a financial adviser. These were usually promoted by, guess who, financial advisers. And they were nearly always mis-sales because the deals were seldom as good as the one you could get in-house. Welcome to pension mis-selling scandal number two. Around 100,000 people were sold the wrong sort of AVC and they have been paid more than £250 million in compensation.

LIVE LONG AND PROSPER

Nowadays pension top-ups are far more likely to be in the form of a personal pension, usually branded 'stakeholder'. Those are explained in the next section. But one word of warning here. Although you are free to put in whatever you like (up to the £215,000 limit) remember that if you have a very good salary and salary-related pension scheme it is theoretically possible you will end up with too much in your pension fund – i.e. more than the £1.5 million allowed (this year; it goes up each year, see Chapter 7). So just make sure that you don't get tempted to put too much into your pension.

And if you are in a decent salary-related pension scheme, you should also ask yourself if you need to save more for a pension. And always buy added years first, if you can.

SALARY SACRIFICE

One of the great money saving wheezes of pensions is 'salary sacrifice'. Generally it saves money for your employer, which is why they are so keen on it. Here is how it works. Say you earn £30,000 and normally you pay 5% of that into your pension. That's £1,500 and leaves you with earnings of £28,500. You pay tax on the latter amount as the pension contribution is tax free. But you still pay National Insurance contributions on all of it, all £30,000, because although National Insurance is an 11% tax on most of your income it does not count as income tax. Mmmm. Work that one out!

So on that £1,500 pension contribution you have paid £1,500 x 11% = £165 in National Insurance. Even worse your employer has paid 12.8%, which is £192.

Just as some religions still sacrifice a goat to appease their gods and avoid disaster, if you sacrifice some salary, the Gods of HM Revenue & Customs are appeased, the disaster of paying that National Insurance is avoided and riches come your way – or at least into your pension fund.

Suppose you and your employer agree that you will be paid not

£30,000 but £28,500. Yep, I know it's a £1,500 pay cut – hence the word 'sacrifice' – but stick with me. Instead of you paying £1,500 into your pension, your employer pays it in for you as their contribution. No tax is due on that and, crucially, no National Insurance contributions either (you may recall that this relief costs £6.8 billion a year but the Treasury doesn't account for it anywhere – see p. 4–5). The same amount goes into your pension but you pay £165 less in National Insurance contributions and your employer pays £192 less. A good employer will pay that saving into your pension so you actually get £1,692 in there. That is your gain from the sacrifice of your pay. But you also lose some things.

★ **Your pay really is less. So you will have a lower salary when it comes to applying for a mortgage, for example. You should explain to the mortgage provider what your 'real' salary is and the deal you have done, but not all will be sympathetic.**
★ **It will affect your death-in-service benefit if you have one. Typically such schemes pay your heirs two, three or four times your salary, which is now less. Your employer could enhance the death-in-service benefit to fill this gap.**
★ **And if you have a salary-related pension scheme, it will affect the salary that is used to work out your pension benefits. The savings are likely to be less here anyway because you will almost certainly be contracted out of the State Second Pension and so your National Insurance contributions – and those paid by your employer – will be lower. In this case, your employer can enhance your pension benefits to cover any shortfall.**

For higher-rate taxpayers, the gain is less as National Insurance contributions fall to 1% on income above £33,540. The percentage gain for the employer is the same though the cash saving will normally be greater. For example, suppose you earn £80,000 a year and pay 10% of your pay into a pension scheme. By sacrificing that £8,000 contribution and earning £72,000, you will save just £80 in the year. But your employer will save up to £1,024. Hopefully they will pass some or all of that saving on to you by way of higher pension contributions.

There are certain formalities to be followed, which is your employer's job not yours. The agreement has to be in writing and irreversible. You as employee cannot unilaterally change your mind. And if the sacrifice is for more than £5,000 a year then the local tax inspector has to be told about the deal. He or she won't stop it. They are just nosey like that.

GROUP PERSONAL PENSIONS

Just to confuse things (well you, actually) a company pension can appear to be a personal pension. If an employer wants to provide a pension but does not want the fuss and responsibility of a full-blown occupational pension scheme, it can offer what is called a 'group personal pension'. This is nothing more than a series of personal pensions for each member of staff who joins. There are two advantages over sorting out your own pension. First the employer will normally pay some money into it, matching your contributions or at least paying a proportion of them. If the employer does not then the main advantage of going with its scheme is lost. Second, because a group personal pension is by its nature going to be bigger business than a pension you buy yourself, the terms may be better. In other words charges may be lower. Or not. So it is important to find out. Personal pensions – including group ones – are of course money-purchase schemes, **not** salary-related schemes.

STAKEHOLDER PENSIONS

Some employers will offer you access to a 'stakeholder' pension. Since October 2001 every employer with more than four employees who does not have a proper occupational pension scheme has to offer its employees at least what is called a stakeholder scheme. (Stakeholder is explained on p. 107. Meanwhile, just read on and hold the question about 'what the ---- does 'stakeholder' mean?') To fulfil that condition the employer has to do a deal with a pension provider to give its employees access to a stakeholder pension and, for those who join, to deduct the contributions to that scheme from their pay.

A stakeholder pension is simply a money-purchase scheme, with the big difference that your employer does not put any money into it. At all. Ever. So if you want 11% of your pay to go in, you have to find it all. And if you want 19% to go in, you still have to find it all. And if you want 25% to go in, guess what? You're on your own. And that is why although almost all employers have to offer one, seven out of ten of them remain empty; no-one has joined. And quite right too. If you want a stakeholder pension, pick your own. More on how to do that later.

CHANGING JOBS

I dealt with this earlier, but in case you are one of those non-serial readers let me just ask you to turn back to p. 30 for the detail. The burden of what I said there is if you do not intend to stay in your current crappy job for long or, as you put it to friends (and your Mum, though she isn't fooled), you expect to move around a lot in your career, it doesn't matter. As long as you are in a job for three months or more (ignore friends who tell you it's two years, it changed in April 2006 to three months) you can take your contributions with you and the ones your employer put in and transfer the lot to another pension scheme, including a personal pension if you want. Or in some cases you can leave them there to grow. Which may or may not be the best idea. But as I said, details on p. 30–31.

Of course paying into numerous pension schemes as your career blossoms and you move from one great job to another (see, you fooled me!) can lead to losing track of them. But don't worry. Those nice people at the Pension Tracing Service keep track of them for you. The service is free and run by the Government. It holds details of more than 200,000 occupational schemes and nowadays it also keeps track of personal pensions of various sorts too. So that great Filing Cabinet in the Sky, known as the internet, has come to the rescue of feckless memory-lapsed individuals once more. How did you get that series of high-powered pensionable jobs, I ask myself.

Nice and helpful as they are, the Pension Tracing Service people will need you to cudgel the little grey cells a bit. So be ready with some details. Because the more information you can give them, the more likely they will be to find an up-to-date contact address for the pension scheme. So write down the full name and address of the employer who ran the pension scheme, and if you know it changed its name at any time or was taken over, that will help too. If all that is too much for you, then perhaps you know what kind of business it was in? What did you do there? And if it was a personal pension, which insurance company ran it? Dates are always useful too. When did you join? When did you leave?

And so on. With any luck the Pension Tracing Service will fill all those embarrassing gaps in your memory – it was such a long time ago, I was just a kid – and track it down. But do remember, even if they do, it may turn out that you left and took your money with you. In the past that was possible, even if you had paid in for as much as five years.

CHAPTER SIX

Your Own Little Pot: The 80s Dream

'The past is a foreign country. They do things differently there.' So begins L P Hartley's book *The Go Between*, a story of illicit sex and the destruction of childhood trust. The plot isn't relevant. And if you want illicit sex, why not mark this page – stop it! – put the book down and then return to it when you can concentrate?

Back in the room? Right. If we go back 20 years to 1986 it *was* a foreign country. I remember it well – a distant dream (or nightmare), with Margaret Thatcher in her ninth year as Prime Minister, Nigella Lawson's Dad as Chancellor and Norman Fowler (who he? ed.) in charge of pensions as Secretary of State for Social Services. Leading the Opposition was Neil Kinnock, and don't say he knew nothing about pensions. As a former MP and EU Commissioner he has retired on an income most of us can only dream of in our working lives, never mind in our retirement.

Anyway, the idea was that pensions would one day be a real problem and so the Government, with rare foresight, would set us all free from our chains and allow anyone to take out a pension of their own. At the time there were good pensions in the civil service (some things are the same everywhere) and in some large companies. In addition a few professionals invested in what were called retirement annuity contracts or section 226 pensions. Much of that money went into a pension fund with Britain's oldest life assurance company, favoured particularly by judges and the legal profession, called Equitable Life. Whoops.

But most people still relied on the state and that included the State Earnings Related Pension Scheme (SERPS) created by Barbara Castle, weakened by her own Cabinet colleagues and then with two hefty blows banged, shorn and quartered, literally, by the Thatcher government. Instead of the poor value (after the changes), uncertain (would you trust politicians, the elected members in Government asked) and in any case unaffordable (they claimed) state scheme, you could now buy your very own portable pension pot. And to make sure it wouldn't arrive empty, you could take some of the contributions you would have paid into the state scheme and pop them in, together with tax relief – which wasn't paid on state scheme contributions – and a nice bonus from the bulging National Insurance Fund. All courtesy of taxpayers in general.

The financial services industry – previously called the insurance business – thought it had woken up in the land of the All-Year Christmas. Teams of poorly trained commission-driven sales staff descended on a hapless population who – encouraged by television adverts showing a man literally bursting out of the chains of state control and newspaper copy which implied that for a few pounds a week anyone could buy political and financial independence – were willingly mis-sold £11.5 billion worth of pensions. Eventually the industry had to spend £2 billion finding the nearly two million people affected and repaying them the £11.5 billion they should never have put into their own pension in the first place. It was just the first in a series of at least five major financial scandals – the fertile soil on which the industry has continued to thrive. See pp. 24–25.

The big innovation was the personal pension – that friendly name replacing the esoteric 's.226 retirement annuity contract' and designed for everyone. It is still with us.

GETTING PERSONAL

A personal pension is just that. Your own little pension pot with your name on it that you pay money into. The kindly old Chancellor adds subsidies. The magic pot is tax proof, so the wicked taxman cannot get near it. And if you leave it in a cupboard, be it ever so dusty, it grows and grows and grows. Thirty years later you have almost forgotten that weird old pot in the cupboard. You feel so tired. Tomorrow is your 60th birthday and you are fed up with working in the mines all day. You are not sure how much longer you can carry your pick and shovel, never mind dig up stuff and carry it out. 'Oh dear!' you sigh 'How can I stop? I will have nothing! How will I eat?' Midnight approaches and you open the cupboard to get out some cider to celebrate your great age. You spy the magic pot! Which you had almost forgotten about. Somehow, today it looks, well, bigger. And, you rub your eyes, is it glowing just a little? Your wipe away the dust and see the letters P E N S. As you try to make out what it says, the old cuckoo clock starts to sing. Cuckoo, cuckoo, cuckoo . . . eight more . . . then cuckOO. Midnight. You really are 60. But wait! The magic pot is cracking open! You see a yellow glint. More cracks. More glints. Gold pours out! You buy yourself a huge pension for life. And there is no longer Sleepy, Sneezy, Grumpy, Doc, Bashful and Dopey. They all become Happy! Ever after.

Such a nice story. And sometimes, just sometimes, it might come true.

The problem is that only one thing about the pot is guaranteed. What you put in it. The others are just tales. It does not always protect the contents from the taxman. The money in it does not always get bigger, sometimes it can shrink. And worst of all, there is a hole in the bottom. And the more you put in, the bigger the hole gets. So whatever you put in and however much the contents grow, some of it drains away every moment of every day of every year.

Let's look at these things separately.

How much you put in is nowadays pretty much up to you. Subject to the maximum of your annual earnings (or £215,000 if you earn more than that) you can put in what you can afford. Even if your earnings are less than £3,600 a year, you are allowed to put in up to £3,600. In fact, you can put in that much even if you have no earnings at all. So someone who inherits money, or is given money, or has interest from money in the bank can put up to £3600 of it into a pension. A parent can even start a pension for a child. So really what you put in is entirely up to you. All you have to decide is how much you can afford – or what you are prepared to give up to afford more.

The rate of return is the tough one. There are no guarantees. And one thing you cannot be told is how much your pension fund will grow each year. Or rather, you will be told but it will not be true. Or it might be true, but if it is that will just be by coincidence. Not just because it is about the future and that is by its nature unpredictable, but because the figures you are shown are nothing to do with the investment itself. They do not reflect what that fund hopes, believes or still less promises will be achieved. They are standard figures laid down by the good old Financial Services Authority and every fund must conform to them. For pensions the figures are 5%, 7% and 9% a year. Sometimes they are called low, medium and high projections – and they are before any charges have been taken off. So 7% a year after charges of 1.5% a year leaves 5.5% a year growth. The only variation from that is if the people who run the fund believe that growth will be less than these amounts, then they can show a lower amount. Few of them do. These standard growth rates were invented some years ago in order to prevent financial services companies exaggerating the rates they expected to get. So they do not reflect anything about the fund where your money is actually invested. They are, like second marriage, the triumph of hope over experience.

HOW MUCH IT LEAKS

Every pension fund has a back door in it. Although the money is yours – and even you can do nothing with it until you retire (except move it to another pension fund) – the pension provider can sneak in through the back door every year and take money out to cover the costs of looking after the fund for you. These annual management charges are measured as a percentage of the size of the fund. So the bigger the fund, the bigger the charge taken out. This can be less than 1% a year of the value of the fund or it can be more than 2.5%. With some funds there will also be charges taken off the money when you first invest it. And if you invest every month or year, that deduction will be made off every new payment into the fund. This initial charge can be 5% of your money. So you write a cheque for £100 and £95 goes into your fund. And the charges don't stop there. If the manager sells anything in the fund or buys more to go in it – which they will have to do every time you invest more – there will be charges for that too. The buying price of a share is always different from the selling price. The difference is called the spread and is typically around 3%. So it is not so much one hole in your pot. It is two or three. Or maybe there is just one back door, but several people have the key.

STAKEHOLDER AT THE HEART

Stakeholder isn't an acronym – though if anyone can make up a good backronym I would like to know it. In fact stakeholder is barely even a word. But if New Labour is anything (a big question in itself), it is the party of neologisms. In my 13-year-old Shorter Oxford English Dictionary a stakeholder is simply 'an independent party with whom each of those who make a wager deposits the money wagered'. And in fact that is a pretty good definition of a pension! 'You give me loads of money and I bet I will give you a decent pension when you retire.' 'Bet you won't.' 'Will too!' 'Won't!' 'Who says?' etc.

Except in this case, one party to the bet keeps all the money. And the other hopes the first will be honest when the time comes to shuffle off their work clothes and begin the years before the mortal coil follows.

The new use of the word 'stakeholder' transforms the noun into an adjective. It is applied to personal pensions which fulfil certain criteria that the Government thinks are a Good Thing. First, the charges are low. There can be no initial charge and the annual management charge cannot be more than 1.5% a year. In other words the provider is allowed to take up to 1.5% of your money every year to run the scheme. Until April 2005 the charge cap was 1%, but after effective lobbying from the financial services industry the Government raised it to 1.5%. That rate applies to the first ten years you pay into the pension – after that it has to fall to no more than 1%. Stakeholder pensions taken out before April 2005 must continue to cap their charges to 1%.

There are other rules on stakeholder charges too. You can stop, restart or change your payments whenever you want without paying a penalty. And if you want to move your money to a different pension provider, the scheme you leave cannot make a charge.

Hang on, would any of them really make charges for those things? Isn't that like Boots charging you if you make your weekly visit and spend £10 rather than £20? Or making you pay if you leave the store without buying anything and decide to shop at Superdrug instead?

Yep. You have got it. Have you ever heard the phrase 'yawning chasm'? That is what lies between the way financial products are sold and the way any other retail market works.

The other amazing thing about stakeholder pensions is that you can start contributions from as little as £20 and have the choice to pay your contribution weekly, monthly or less frequently. Welcome to my shop. Spend as much or as little as you like. And if you find a better deal over the road, take it. No wonder the financial services industry hates stakeholder products. It's just like running a grocer's. Thin margins and lots of long hours.

TAX SUBSIDY

I've said it before and I will probably say it again but every taxpayer in the UK, in or out of a pension, subsidises the pensions the rest of us pay into. That is because every penny we pay into a pension is not taxed. If tax has already been paid on it then we are given it back. The cost of this subsidy is officially put at £12.3 billion in 2004/05. But there are reasons to put it a lot higher, certainly £19 billion and arguably more than £27 billion. As it is hard to imagine any of those numbers except to know that they are really really very big indeed, the exact amount probably doesn't matter. But it is huge. If it was abandoned the Chancellor could knock 3½p, 5½p or 8p off the basic rate of tax. See pp.4–5 for details.

Most of this money – about 55% – goes to 2.5 million people who earn enough to pay the higher rate of tax and contribute to a pension. The rest, about 45%, goes to 13 million others who pay the basic rate of tax. The remaining 13 million people who pay income tax but do not pay into a pension get nothing. They would probably rather pay less tax than spend it on subsidising the better off to make sure they stay that way in retirement.

I've mentioned A-Day a few times. It's the day – 6 April 2006 – when the 50 years of rules about how much and how we could invest in pensions were swept away. No-one in the Government has ever explained why it was called A-Day. We are about to find out.

First, a word about tax relief – what it means and how it works for pensions. If you earn money you pay tax (well, as long as you earn more than £5,035). And if you don't then paying into a pension is not really a priority. The basic rate of tax is 22%. In other words you earn £100 and the taxman takes £22 of it. Just to complicate things there is a lower rate of tax (10%) which is charged on the first chunk you earn above your £5,035 allowance – the chunk was £2,095 in 2005/06. But for pensions we can blessedly ignore this. Money put into your pension is not taxed. So if you put in £100 that you have already paid tax on, the Chancellor gives you back the tax you have paid. He does that by paying that amount into your pension. Now you might think if you put in £100 he will put in £22. But no. Remember this £100 has already had the tax deducted. So how much do you have to earn to have £100 left after tax at the basic rate? Well it's not £122. If you multiply that by 22% you get £26.84 and take that away from £122 you get £95.16. No. You need to earn £128.20 to have £100 left. (Here is the sum: £128.20 x 0.22 = £28.20, leaving you with £100). So if you put £100 into a pension the Chancellor gives you back the £28.20 tax you've paid on it. He does that by paying that much into your pension. You pay in £100 he pays in £28.20.

Now he does this whatever rate of tax you pay. So if your income is very low and you pay no tax, then you still get it. Anyone can put £3,600 into a pension scheme. This means that you can put in £2,808 and the Chancellor puts in £792 tax relief *even if you pay no tax*. If your income is low enough that you only pay tax at 10%, you still get it. If you pay basic rate tax, of course you get it. But if you are lucky enough to pay tax at the higher 40% rate, you get even more.

Now suppose you are a higher-rate tax payer. The same thing happens. To earn £100 after tax, you have to have earned £166.67. (Work it out. £166.67 × 40% = £66.67, leaving you £100.) But the arithmetic gets a bit tricksy. You pay in £100 and the Chancellor returns the basic rate tax – £28.20 – into your pension fund. But you are a *higher-rate* tax payer. So you have paid in £128.20 after basic rate tax of 22%. The other 18% (40 − 22 = 18) is then reclaimed by you on your self-assessment form at the end of the tax year. So you get back £23.07. This all works out because you have then paid in £100 − £23.07 = £76.93, and had total tax relief of £23.07 + £28.20 = £51.27. Which is exactly 66.65% of the £76.93 the contribution cost you. (I know. I had to go through it a couple of times too. But it is right.)

So pensions are very generous to higher-rate taxpayers. And it gets better. Here are some more numbers. I know, I know you hate numbers and arithmetic. But look at it this way. The money that you have is measured in one way – numbers. How much is in your pocket? Nothing? Twenty quid? A hundred? They're just numbers. And these numbers will amaze you. You start with two empty pockets. You put £20 in your right hand pocket, but when you take it out there's £25.64. And a bit later, you discover someone has put £4.62 in your empty left hand pocket as well!

You are a higher-rate taxpayer and aged at least 50 (or 55 if you are reading this after April 2010). You write a cheque for £7,800 made out to 'My New Pension'. Immediately the Chancellor gets out his cheque book and writes out one to 'Your New Pension' for £2,200 making the total contribution into your pension £10,000. At the end of the tax year you can claim back the higher-rate tax you have paid, so when you do your tax return Gordon slashes your bill by £1,800. So you have spent £6,000 and in your new pension is £10,000.

Now, you are already over the age when you can 'retire'. Remember that doesn't mean you have to stop work. It doesn't mean you have to do anything really. But it does mean you can say, 'Oh. There is £10,000 in my new pension.' You say the magic words. No, not abracadabra but Benefit Crystallisation Event—see p.165. (A relative of a friend of mine actually thought the magic word was 'veryise' – her hero, the comic conjurer Tommy Cooper, used to say he'd do a trick before 'your very eyes'.) Immediately you say that, you can take 25% of your new pension fund as cash. So you write to Your New Pension and ask for that and they send you a cheque for £2,500. That means there is £7,500 in your pension fund and it has now cost you £6,000 − £2,500 = £3,500. Net profit £4,000.

You can leave that £7,500 in your pension for when you really want to retire. Though you won't be able to take another 25% of it, you will be able to take 25% of the difference between what it is worth now and what it will be worth then when you take a second Benefit Crystallisation Event. And you can do this as often as you like as long as you have the money to do it and of course stay within the contributions limit and the lifetime pension fund limit. Those are all explained in the next chapter.

But it gets better. Suppose you take the £2,500 you have got back in tax-free cash and pay that into your pension. The same arithmetic applies. You put in £2,500, the Chancellor tops it up at once with £705.13 tax relief at the basic rate and sends you a cheque for £576.92 higher-rate tax relief. So there is another £3,205 in your pension, you have a cheque for nearly £577 and of course you can, if you wish, take out £801.28 in tax-free cash! Which you can also recycle. . . . We are in the wonderful world of iteration, or as a computer programmer might say, repeat until zero. The amounts come down each time by about 70% so by about the sixth or seventh iteration become a bit trivial (by iteration 13 you are writing an extra cheque for 1p to your pension!). But if you do a total of the whole lot – remembering you initially wanted to put £7,800 into your pension – then it turns out that you can put in £11,479.25; claim back £3,679.25 tax-free cash, claim your tax reliefs of course, and you end up paying £5,150.94 for a pension fund which starts off at £11,037.74.

Roughly speaking you can safely write a cheque for twice the amount you want to put into your pension. Almost that amount will end up in your pension. And you will get half of it back.

If you are reading this wearing an anorak, here is that paragraph again in precise terms.

You can safely write a cheque for $2^8/_{35}$ of the amount you want to put into your pension: $^{25}/_{26}$ of that amount will end up in your pension. And you will get $^7/_{15}$ of it back.

So. Decide how much you can afford this year to put into your pension. Multiply that by 2.23 and write a cheque for that amount. You will get more than half of that back through tax-free cash and higher-rate tax relief. But at the end of the day your pension will be almost as much as that original cheque.

It's arithmetic Jim, but not as we know it. And at last we know what the 'A' in 'A-Day' stands for – 'Amazing-tax-breaks-for-the-rich-Day'.

But hang on a minute. The arithmetic works quite well even for basic rate taxpayers. It is not as good of course, you don't get that £23 back for every £100 you initially pay in. But it is still like producing money out of a hat. You write a cheque for £780. The Chancellor boosts that by £220, so there is £1,000 in your pension. You take out £250 tax-free cash, leaving you £750 in your pension. And it has cost you just £530. Veryise! And this arithmetic works even for people who pay no tax at all, as anyone can put at least £3,600 into their pension in each tax year.

One word of warning. Flash Gordon has stepped in to save the Universe from abuse of this recycling stuff. You can still get away with recycling as long as you fulfil ANY of the following three conditions:

★ The total amount of pension lump sum you take in a year is £15,000 or less.
★ Your increased contributions are no more than a fifth of the lump sum.
★ Your annual pension contributions do not increase by more than a 'significant amount', which will also be about a fifth.

And even if you *do* break one of these rules, you will not be caught as long as you did not intend to recycle when you took out the lump sum. Though proving that might be difficult. Especially now you've read these paragraphs!

Now, we are coming to another cunning plan. If your total pension fund is £15,000 or less, you can take it out in cash (see pp. 142–144). Normally a quarter is tax free and the rest is taxed. But if you pay no tax, then it is all tax free. So if you are a non-earning partner aged at least 56 who pays no tax and has (or some kind person will lend you) around £10,000 saved up in the bank, here is how you can turn that into around £15,000 in just over four years.

★ 6 April 2006. Start a pension invested in fixed rate bonds paying 5% a year. Pay in £2,808. Chancellor tops it up with £792 making £3,600 (the most you are allowed). Immediately take out 25% tax-free cash. So £2,700 in the fund and it has cost you just £1,908.
★ 6 April 2007. Your fund has grown by 5%. Repeat above.
★ 6 April 2008. Ditto.
★ 6 April 2009. Ditto.
★ 6 April 2010. Ditto. By now you are over 60. So you apply at once for commutation of your trivial fund. It is worth £14,919. You get a quarter tax-free and the rest taxed at your marginal rate. Which is zero. So you pay no tax.

For a net outlay of 5 x £1,908 = £9,540 you now have £14,919 in the bank – a profit of £5,379. And no risk. Of course by then the limit for a fund that is considered 'trivial' will probably be at least £18,500, and you could safely let the scheme run another year if you wanted and you had the money to lay out. Then the figures could show that you had put in £11,448 and taken out £18,365, a profit of nearly £7,000 over five years. Veryise! But see the warning above about the Chancellor.

So that is the tax subsidy. Risk-free, public money boosting every penny you put into your pension.

> ### Rule of Prosperity
>
> If you can't pay into a company pension then pay into a personal one. If you don't you are volunteering to pay more tax.

INVESTING YOUR PENSION

You will need help to decide where to invest your pension. And for that you will need an independent financial adviser (IFA). You can find out all about them – more than they would like you to know – in Chapter 10. Here we look at the basics of what you have to decide. If you want something a bit racier than ordinary pension investments then the SIPP section below is probably for you (if only as a warning not to be so silly and to turn back and read this).

You might think that your financial adviser would tell you how to invest your pension. But no. Your IFA will say to you something like, 'What is your attitude to risk?' Here is how the conversation might go.

IFA: 'What is your attitude towards risk?

YOU: 'What do you mean?'

IFA, smiling: 'Investment risk. It works like this. The bigger the risk you take, the bigger the reward. Now I could put all your money in the bank. That's safe, but frankly you'd be lucky if that kept up with inflation. So at the end of the day your pension fund wouldn't even be worth the same as when you put the money in. That's not very clever is it?'

YOU, filling the pause: 'No, I suppose not. What's the alternative?'

IFA: 'The risk–reward ratio means that if you want a bigger return you have to take a bigger risk. So you might invest in the stock market. That means there is a bit of risk, but your investment has the potential for much higher growth.'

YOU: 'Right.'

IFA: 'So. Are you prepared to take a bit of risk, to get potentially a bigger reward?'

YOU: 'Yes, I guess so.'

Now, you've both made mistakes here. The IFA has used the word 'potentially' to cover his arse. He didn't promise you anything. That was of course not a mistake. It was careful training. But he did use the time-honoured phrase 'if you want a bigger return you have to take a bigger risk'. At this point you might ask yourself (or indeed him): if taking a risk means you get a bigger reward, where is the risk? Indeed, what is the risk? It's a useful question to remember. It flummoxes all but the best.

If you want to cross the road as quickly as you can, then you can take a bit of a risk and just run across without looking. Most of the time you will get there quicker. Some of the time you will end up as a red smear on the tarmac. That's risk and reward. So what is the risk of an investment based around shares?

Does it mean you might get back less than you would have got in the bank? Yes.

Does it mean you might even get back less than you put in? Yes.

Does it mean, erm, you might get back a lot less than you put in? Yes.

Does it mean, gulp, you might get back half what you put in? Yes.

Does it mean, cold sweat, you might get back nothing? Yes.

That is the risk. And the riskier the investment, the bigger the chance that you will move down that list of risks.

So what is the plus side? After all, you are risking having less in retirement than if you put the money in the bank. The plus side is that money invested in shares over the long term has grown faster than money invested in bonds, or gilts, or cash. According to Barclays Capital which looks at these things over every 20-year period from 1900, money invested in shares has done better than the other two. And before you ask, we don't know about property because no-one has measured it over that period. The reason for that is the financial services industry is devoted to shares and it does not want too many people putting their money in property. There simply isn't enough of it to go round. That's why at the end of October 2005 Standard Life said it would no longer accept new investments in its two property funds, including its £2.7-billion commercial property pension fund. There just was not enough high quality property around to buy with any new money that came in.

It is the only part of the retail market where the customer has to make such difficult decisions. You go into Comet to buy a fridge.

'How cold do you want it?'

'Well, I hadn't really thought, I was more interested in colour, really, I rather like blue, dark blue. And I want a cold drinks dispenser. And it has to fit a gap that is about oh that wide. Hang on a minute, I wrote it down; here it is – 580mm.'

'Yes, but how cold?'

'Well, cold enough to keep things fresh.'

'If only it was that easy, madam. I could sell you 8°C. But I wouldn't be doing my job. Because you might prefer 5°C or even 2°C. Or maybe you would like 10°C? It all depends what sort of risk you want to take that your food will go off? The bigger the risk the higher the reward – it costs less to buy, less to run. The lower the risk the more you have to pay.'

Strangely before you went into Comet you didn't research the temperature that food needs to be kept at, nor what happens if it is not. So you haven't got a clue whether it needs to be a cucumber-solidifying 2°C or a milk-churning 12°C. You are not a food specialist. But until you state the temperature, the salesperson will not sell you a fridge. So you stick with the plastic bag tied round the outside handle of the window.

In the financial world they are more sophisticated. If you really don't know what attitude to risk you have, or even if you say you don't want to risk your savings going down, still less plummeting, the answer will be, 'I'll put you down as low to medium shall I? That normally suits most people.' And then he (it is normally a 'he') will carry on to recommend putting your money into a stock market investment. A favourite type of question is, 'are you very cautious, more balanced, or perhaps want to take a bit of a chance with things?' Very few will say 'very cautious'. Some will say 'balanced' – it sounds sensible doesn't it? And a surprising number will admit to 'taking a bit of a chance'. After all they do the lottery. Ideal answers for any IFA to recommend whatever they want.

> In a mystery shopping exercise done in April 2003 for BBC Radio 4's *Money Box Investigates*, our shopper had inherited £76,000 from his mum which he said he wanted to invest for his own pension, but would be very upset if he lost any of it. He was put as low to medium or medium risk by most of the 22 financial advisers he went to see and generally advised to invest it in products where his money could be lost, though that often wasn't made clear to him.

So when your IFA asks you your attitude to risk, remember that risk does not mean higher rewards. It means you might get higher rewards than sticking it in the bank but you might get lower ones than sticking it under the mattress. That is what risk is. You might lose some or all of your money.

SHARES, BONDS AND CASH

In truth the risk you normally take with a pension fund is that it will be disappointing. Ordinary, bog standard, reasonable, average, boringly OK, these are all *good* terms for a pension – because what you don't want are surprises. OK it would be nice if your pension fund was worth more than you expect. But it would not be good if it was worth a lot less. After all that saving and scrimping, you do not want to end up about £20 a week better off than your neighbour who has never saved a penny.

We are now leaving the thickets of confusion, where you can at least chop yourself a clear path, and heading into the marshes of complexification. In these swampy areas words do not mean what they say. Arithmetic does not add up. And as for promises, well, I think you'll find that what you thought was a promise or at least a guarantee and if not that then surely at least a commitment, was in fact nothing of the kind. It was at best an aspiration, a hope. Don't bring your waders. They won't be long enough. A snorkel might help. And a thick skin.

When you buy 'a pension' you are buying a part of a fund, a big fund, or parts of several very big funds. Those funds could be invested in all sorts of things which we'll come to in a minute. But there will generally be someone in charge of these funds who will be extremely well paid and he or she (a few are women) will be supported by a large team of highly-paid people with a bigger team of very well-paid people reporting to them. Running pension funds is expensive. These managers are watching the world markets, studying companies, talking to people, dashing about, discussing their findings, making decisions, buying stuff, selling other stuff, all with one view in mind – to make that fund grow. Some of that growth will come from dividends or interest but most of it will probably come from buying low and selling dear.

All these people and the offices they work in and the people who support them cost a lot of money. Your money. Because they are paid out of the charges made to your fund. Those charges will drain out of the little hole in your pension pot whether the fund inside it grows or shrinks.

There are thousands of funds that your pension could be invested in. They come with names that sound like promises such as Higher Income, Initial Growth, Wealthbuilder, High Yield Corporate Bond. Some are designed to appeal to your personality like Cautious Managed, UK Aggressive, Overseas Tactical, Strategic Bond, SafetyFirst. Others imply good things such as Asia Pacific Leaders, UK Alpha, Selected Opportunities, Liontrust. You will find a lot of 'balanced' funds, a sprinkling of 'global', a fair few 'opportunities', and of course lots of 'income' and 'growth' funds.

Every single one of these names is meaningless. Well, OK if a fund has the word 'Japanese' in its title then quite of bit of the money will be held in Japan. If it is called 'smaller companies' then it should have a large chunk of its money invested in the not-so-large sector. But aside from those matters of fact most of the words are 'hopes', 'aspirations', 'intentions' or 'aims'. If a growth fund shrinks, an income fund produces none or a wealthbuilder leaves you poorer, you cannot complain. Or rather you can and probably will (I would), but it will almost certainly get you nowhere. Because the small – nowadays not-so-small – print will have made it clear that a name is just a name and describes hopes and intentions, not (heaven forbid) promises. In the City the gentlemen's word is not their boring old bond. It is usually something far more risky.

But in this impenetrable jargon you do find words that you should note. Some funds are 'managed' others are 'trackers'. That is a big difference. More in a moment. Some have the word 'bonds' or 'cash' and we'll come to those. But first let's deal with shares.

Skip this paragraph if you really know what a share is. A share is literally a share in a company. A very tiny share admittedly – perhaps a billionth. But when you have a share, you do own that bit of the company. It gives you very little power – you may get the power to vote if you own the share directly, but not if you own it through a fund. But a billionth of, say, Vodafone is good to have.

That share can make you money in two ways. First the company will pay you a share of the profits it makes each year. Most of the profits will usually be what is called 'retained' so they can be used for investment, perhaps for buying another company or maybe just to sit in the bank as rainy-day money. If the company has a salary-related pension scheme it may have to use a chunk of its profits to pay down the deficit. But some of it will be divided up among shareholders. And if you own a billionth of that company, you will get a billionth of that money. Overall the dividends on the shares in big UK companies represent a return of just over 3% at the end of 2005. In other words, if you owned £100 worth of shares spread across the FTSE 100 companies, you will get dividends worth about £3.19. Not bad. But not great. You could earn more in the bank.

> For example, suppose you own 22 shares in Britain's biggest company, BP. There are about 22 billion shares in BP so you own one billionth of the company. In 2004 BP made profits of around £8.6 billion. But it kept most of that for investment and distributed about £3.8 billion to its shareholders. That amounted to around 16p for each share. So your 22 shares would bring income of £3.52. Now suppose you bought them in January 2003 when they cost around £4 each. Your 22 shares would have cost £88, so a dividend in 2004 of £3.52 is a return of 4%, which is good.

But there is a second way that you earn money from shares. They grow in value. So shares you bought for £100 this year may be worth £110 next year – which is 10% growth. As well as the dividends. The value of shares in one company goes up and down just as the price of peas goes up and down. If Jamie Oliver suggests making tasty pea and potato soup with a sprig of parsley, demand for peas rises, and so does the price. When people get bored with it, demand plummets, the supermarkets are left with too many peas and sell them off cheap. Some things that make share prices rise and fall are sensible – the company's profits, changes at the top, a growing demand for what it makes. Others are less clear – the City is just said to have lost confidence in it and the price falls, or maybe thinks a takeover is possible so the price rises. Technically the price of shares in a company is supposed to represent the value at today's prices of future profits. But, fuelled by greed and damped down by fear, the market often doesn't work like that.

> By September 2005 your 22 BP shares would have reached a price of more than £6.80 each so you could have sold them for around £150 – a profit of more than £60. But if you had bought them a year earlier, the price would have been well over £6 then. And if you had sold them at their low of around £3.70 in early 2003, you would have lost around £50. So timing is everything. And of course some shares fall and never rise again.

Because shares in any single company are very volatile – they go up and down – the general health of the UK business world is usually judged by the shares in big groups of companies. The movements in shares in these groups of companies are measured by an index. If overall the prices rise, so does the index. The favourite in the UK is called the FTSE 100 and represents the change in price of the shares in the biggest hundred companies in the UK. It started off at 1,000 in 1984 and as I write is 5,501. Which means that the price of shares in this index has risen about five and a half times since then. The problem with the FTSE is that the biggest companies make the biggest change. At the moment three of the ten biggest are oil companies, BP and Royal Dutch Shell A and B account for nearly a fifth of the value of the FTSE100. The top ten companies in the FTSE100 account for half the index and the top 20 account for two thirds. So by looking at the FTSE100 and how it moves, you are really looking at the movement in the share prices of these twenty companies.

A broader index is the FTSE All Share, though you will struggle to find that value mentioned anywhere. It is not the index of all the shares on the London Stock Exchange but the ones that are easy to buy and sell – which is around 700 companies. This index is more representative of the value of UK companies – it contains more than 98% by value of the publicly-owned companies in the UK. Another index is the FTSE 250 which uses the 250 biggest companies under the top 100. And of course there is an index called the FTSE350 which is the FTSE100 and the FTSE250 combined.

But when people (and I tentatively include myself in that category) say 'share prices rose by . . .' or less precisely just 'shares fell by . . .' or the City report comes to an end with 'the FTSE is up 25 at fifty three twenty one', we normally mean the FTSE 100. Not because it's the best but because (a) you need one measure and (b) well, we are only human.

You need to know all this (and if you skipped to here go back and read it) because there are two kinds of fund that invest in shares. One kind is run by all those expensive managers I mentioned a few paragraphs ago, using their skill and ability to pick and choose shares that are going to rise in value and buying them before they do and spotting those that are on the way down and selling them in good time. If they do it right you will make a lot of money. But if not, you will make less and might lose some of it. These are called managed funds.

The second sort of fund doesn't worry about all that difficult stuff. It just buys shares to imitate one of the indexes, such as the FTSE 100 or the FTSE All Share. And as the index rises and falls so does your investment, if the fund has done its job well. The theory is that if all the experts are right and over the long term shares produce a better return than anything else (and that is after all measured by the whole stock market or the FTSE100), tracking that index is an easy way to hitch your investment wagon to that winning horse. And of course it is a lot cheaper than the managed funds. Shadowing an index is not a trivial task, it's actually quite technical and involves computers; but it is much easier than predicting what will go up and what will come down. That requires a crystal ball. And they are much more expensive and less reliable than a special offer at PC World.

I could stop here, because I think for beginners and for cautious-ish people a FTSE All Share tracker is the best way to go with your pension money – it may not make you spectacular gains, but you take relatively little risk. As long as you buy in to the belief that investments in shares do better in the long term than anything else that your pension fund might be invested in.

All trackers are not the same. You can get a tracker to follow most major indexes. If you want you can follow foreign indexes, London indexes, specialist indexes – and it might be a good idea to have some of your money doing that. But the most important thing is the cost. Trackers should be cheap. You can get ones that charge as little as 0.1% of your fund. That compares to 1% or 1.5% for many others and even higher charges for non-stakeholder pensions. You have to be careful about charges. The figure you should look at is not the annual management charge – that's what is quoted above – but something called the Total Expense Ratio or TER. That takes account of (almost) all the charges the fund makes such as management, administration, fees, subsidies and custody (a posh name for looking after the documents that show you own shares of bonds or other items. In the UK, most of these documents are now held electronically so all that custody requires is a reference by your name relating to electronic entitlement. So, yes, they mean filing. And they charge you for it). For the Fidelity fund it is about 0.35% a year of your money. Still cheap, in fact just about the cheapest. And given that all trackers should do the same job – though some are better at it than others – you might as well just go on price. But do make sure it tracks the index accurately.

One word of warning about Total Expense Ratios. They do not cover everything. Most stuff, yes. But commission, may not be included. That can just drain way, sight–unseen, before the return on your fund is calculated. If it's not complexification, it is certainly opacification. I made that word up. Great, isn't it?

TRACKER CRACKERS

I am a fan of trackers because of what they achieve. They let you hitch your pension wagon to the reliable old horse that trots up and down the hills of stock market growth . . . OK, OK I'll stop that metaphor there, but you know what I mean. However there are problems with trackers. They can be expensive and some do not do even their simple little job that well. There is an alternative called Exchange Traded Funds, and sorry but I will call them ETFs for now. ETFs are cheap and efficient but they are generally not recommended by financial advisers, because ETFs do not pay them any commission. Not even the small amount that trackers pay. So you may well not be recommended them – but they track the market, do it well and are cheap.

ETFs are marketed in the UK by a number of firms. They are shares in a fund and are bought and sold like any other share. However, there is no spread on the price so the buying price is the same as the selling price. And, unlike normal shares, there is no stamp duty. That helps keep the costs down. Typically you will pay ½% a year or less in management fees.

You can buy ETFs that follow various FTSE indexes, as well as indexes that follow other markets.

So that's it. Pension sorted. Buy a cheap ETF that tracks the UK market.

'Hang on, hang on' you say. 'What about managed funds? What about top quartile performers for each of the last five years? What about growth figures, past performance, asset allocation and diversification? What about bonds – corporate and otherwise? What, Mr Cautious, about cash?'

Well, OK. But quickly.

MANAGED FUNDS

The debate rages about whether trackers or managed funds are best. Every year some managed funds do a lot better than trackers. And every year even more managed funds do worse. When I say 'do better/worse', I mean make more/less money for you.

Let's take something fairly simple: funds that invest across companies in the UK. Do they beat the FTSE All Share index? In other words if you just invested blindly in shares in the 700 companies in that index in the right proportions, would you make more money?

Research by stockbrokers Bestinvest examined 194 such managed funds. In 2004/05 just 35% of them did better than a monkey with a pin. Well, OK, a monkey that invested in the right proportions in the FTSE All Share. In other words, nearly two thirds used their skill and judgement to make their customers less money than an automatic tracker would do.

So why not invest in one of the 35% that did better? If the skill and judgement of those well-paid but very clever folk running these top managed funds can make more money for you, why not go with them? Finding out about last year's performance is relatively easy. It's published in magazines such as *Money Marketing*. Hindsight is a wonderful thing (in fact Lipper, one of the best-known companies that produces past performance figures, calls its service 'Hindsight'). It can tell you where you ought to have invested last year. But what you want to know is where to invest your money this year or next. We could all make money if we could bet on last year's Grand National. But does last year's winner tell you where you should invest for the future? I think not.

One place you will not find past performance figures is in the tables produced by the Financial Services Authority. It has now imposed very strict rules about the use of past performance figures after research it commissioned showed that past performance is no guide to future performance. Funnily enough you hardly ever see it quoted in adverts now.

Actually, the research showed that past *good* performance is no guide to the future. This year's star cannot be expected to do well next year. But it did find that this year's dunce is more likely to be in the corner next year than in the top set. So while bad performance persists, good performance does not.

So what about the 35% of funds which did better in 2004/05? Bestinvest looked further back, and found that out of the 194 funds just 9 had beaten the FTSE All Share index in each of the past five years. And if you go back eight years then none of them had outperformed every year.

But that doesn't mean that all the money spent on the expertise and knowledge of fund managers is wasted. If you look at the performance of the 136 funds that have been around for ten years, about three out of ten have done better than the FTSE All Share taking those ten years as a whole. So although not a single one has done better every single year, if you give them ten years and hang on in the years when you do worse than the index, then 41 out of those 136 will make you more money than in a tracker. But this is all hindsight. It may not help you choose the fund that is going to carry on beating the index. This is the kind of arithmetic and information that a good financial adviser should present you with so you can make what appears to be a rational choice.

But me? I would stick with an Exchange Traded Fund that tracks a FTSE index.

PROPERTY AND OTHER STUFF

The next question you asked was about 'asset allocation'. This is the latest buzz phrase in investment. It's a pompous version of 'don't put all your eggs in one basket' – especially when it's your nest egg. Investing your pension across 700 companies in the UK is a broad basket, but it is still one container. So you should consider what they call other 'asset classes', by which they mean classes of assets not classes about assets (though a lot of Independent Financial Advisers could do with those).

Because for many IFAs diversification means something in the Far East, something in small companies, something in 'special situations' (don't laugh, three of the nine funds that beat the FTSE All Share for five years have 'special situations' in the title. But to me, they sound like one of the fanciful names the science fiction writer Iain M Banks gives to the omniscient artificial intelligences he calls 'spaceship minds'), and something in blue chips. In other words all in shares – so all in the same type of basket.

Real diversification means putting some of your fund outside shares in bonds, some in property, some in commodities (gold, oil, coffee), some in cash. The idea is that you offset the volatility of shares (volatility means the price can change quickly and dramatically) with the steadiness of bonds. And you can put some money in commodities which are considered 'counter-cyclical'. That means that when shares and cash are doing badly people put their trust in solid stuff like gold, oil (OK it's a liquid, but a barrel of it is pretty solid) and aluminium. So commodities run counter to the cycle in shares as they soar and plummet.

In that sense, asset allocation is a *Good Idea*. Doing it is a bit more difficult. Especially with a small amount of money. And the consequence of protecting yourself against risk in any way is that you end up with an overall gain that tends towards the overall growth in the world economy, which is much the same as the gain you will get on cash. In other words if you take out all the risk by perfect diversification, you get an ordinary return. But at least you don't get a nasty loss. It's a bit like mixing up all the colours on a palette – you end up with a kind of brown. It's not very pretty but it does cover the walls.

Here's a quick guide to other asset classes:

Corporate bonds – IFAs will often tell you that corporate bonds are less risky than shares. Indeed one adviser in the *Money Box* mystery shopping exercise described them like this: 'in a low-risk category we have our corporate bond fund – this is the one that invests in cash, fixed interest, things like that – basically with full protection of your capital'. Forget that. It is all nonsense. A corporate bond is a contract with a company. You give them your money and the company promises to give you a fixed, guaranteed rate of interest each year and then at a fixed date in the future to return your money. Corporate bonds are less risky than shares. But there is always the risk that the company will not fulfil its bargain. It might go bust and then you would not get all your money back, perhaps none of it.

Just as you do not buy individual shares, so you should not buy one corporate bond. You can put your pension in a corporate bond fund. This will be invested in bonds from many firms. There will be some very safe ones from companies that no-one expects to get into difficulties, some from more risky ones and some perhaps from flaky companies which may or not survive. The reason for putting some of the fund (yes, yes, some of your money) at risk is simple. These bonds from less well established companies will pay a higher return on your money. After all no-one in their right mind would pick them if there was no advantage. It's the price they pay you for risking your money. Overall the bond fund manager hopes to pick bonds that will pay a higher return but not go horribly wrong. You can also buy an Exchange Traded Fund (ETF— see p. 124) in corporate bonds.

So corporate bonds are less risky than shares but they are not, by any means, risk-free.

Government bonds on the other hand can be completely risk free – at least as long as government-as-we-know-it survives. The downside is that the return is not that high. You can buy these direct and if you had a SIPP (Self-Invested Personal Pension), for example, you could choose to put UK Government Stock, also called 'gilts', in it. But again you are probably going to do it through a fund with a manager (despite the costs that implies). At the moment there is no ETF in UK Government bonds, though you can buy one in German bonds.

Cash – the same goes for cash. There are pension funds that invest your money simply in cash, like a savings account with a bank. These cash funds are not in one account. The manager will keep the money in a variety of places and do the hard work for you of moving it around. Don't expect returns to be wonderful. But there won't be any losses.

Gold, frankincense and myrrh – precious stuff, also known as commodities, is becoming more popular as an investment. Of course there have always been those who swore that palladium was not just a Sunday entertainment, aluminium was not a lightweight investment, or that coffee woke up a sleepy portfolio. By the end of 2005 the price of platinum had risen by 130% over four years (compared with around 4% for shares) to reach a 25-year high. Platinum, like many precious metals, is widely used in industry, especially in catalytic converters on motor vehicles. But of course the phrase '25 year high' means that in 1980 the price was the same as it is now. So beware of talked up commodities.

In fact commodities funds are seldom invested in the products themselves. So there isn't a pension fund storehouse with barrels of oil, bars of gold and sacks of coffee. They buy 'futures' in commodities – see box – or sometimes shares in businesses that deal in the commodities, such as mining companies. Though those are generally to be avoided (remember the old City definition that a gold mine is a hole in the ground with dirt at the bottom and a fool at the top). Although you can buy shares in Exchange Traded Gold, which tracks the value of one tenth of an ounce of gold on the markets. But there will always be dealing charges and the spread between the buying and selling price to pay.

FUTURES' PAST

A 'future' is a contract to buy or sell something at a future date. You do not have to own it at any stage. But you have to honour that contract even if you make a thumping great loss. If you agree to buy a tonne of cocoa for £830 in three months' time and by then the price is £800, you have lost £30 a tonne. But if the price is £850 then you have made £20 and someone else has lost £20. The futures market developed in Liverpool in the 19th century. Cotton was grown thousands of miles away and the long sea journey meant that its price could change between purchase and arrival. Dealers started trading in the 'future' price of cotton to reduce the risk of the price changing. When the American Civil War of 1860–65 disrupted the flow of cotton from the USA to Europe, the price and delivery became even more uncertain. Brokers in Liverpool developed standard contracts for cotton which was due to be delivered in the future. These contracts were then themselves traded, and soon speculators were making more money from trading in the promise of cotton than they ever did buying and selling the bolls themselves. The futures market was born.

Commercial Property – is things like offices, warehouses, shopping centres and industrial units. Over the last five years returns on property funds have generally been positive, right through the time when shares were plummeting. As the people in white coats have to say on toothpaste adverts, I am not a dentist, but I do like investments in property. It is a finite resource with a growing demand.

And that is even more true for:

Domestic Property – With a growing population, more people living by themselves and too few homes being built to cope with that demand, domestic property seems to me a one-way bet. But don't expect to find any funds invested in flats and houses at the moment though that may change because of. . . .

REITs – A new sort of investment called Real Estate Investment Trusts will begin in the next year or so. REITs are big business in the USA, popular in France and Japan, and they will probably become big here too. REITs can invest in commercial or domestic property and there will undoubtedly be some that specialise in different things. The details still have to be worked out but they do promise to give UK investors the first chance to put money into domestic property without actually buying a second home. The relationship between REITs and pensions is not clear but there seems no reason why a pension scheme should not be able to invest in a REIT. A lot of companies are busy selling the idea of REITs and you should be very cautious about charges and risk before you put any of your pension money in a REIT: wait until they have settled down.

You can get asset allocation inexpensively now using Exchange Traded Funds – the ETFs mentioned earlier. You can buy them in just about all these asset classes except domestic property (though REITS will almost certainly change that in the long run). So if you want to move beyond tracking the UK stock market, using the low cost, diversity and flexibility of ETFs is a very good way to do it.

SIPPs (SELF-INVESTED PERSONAL PENSIONS)
It was like watching a juggernaut taking a mountain bend too fast and slowly turning over as it heads for the precipice, leaving havoc in its wake. I am talking of course about the bandwagon labelled SIPPs, which was travelling with a stately certainty towards the drop; all we thought we could do was watch through half-closed eyes and wince for the souls on board as it passed the point where braking would no longer stop it. It was so clearly a mis-selling scandal in the making. And this time no-one could say we didn't know, or couldn't have predicted it. But just as it seemed the 42 tonne artic was past the point of no return, Flash Gordon appeared from nowhere in his spacecraft and prevented disaster.

Let me explain. A Self-Invested Personal Pension is, as you might guess, a kind of personal pension which is – guess what? – self invested. This means that you, the person paying into it, decide absolutely where your money is invested. OK, so it's not 'self-invested' at all, but this is pension talk. We'll have to live with it. SIPPs have been around for some time and until the A-Day changes, you could only choose to invest your SIPP in traditional pension assets like unit trusts, shares, bonds and commercial property such as offices and shops. But all those crazy old-fashioned rules were due to be swept away from April 2006 allowing works of art, houses and, well, just about anything to be put into a SIPP. The danger was that a SIPP as such is not regulated: anyone can set one up. There has to be a SIPP trustee, which must be a regulated financial company such as a bank or insurance company, but they tend to operate in a hands-off way and some consider that their job is simply to ensure that the SIPP conforms with the law – and no more. Within that constraint, they will allow any sort of legal investment to be put into a SIPP. So the plans to take restrictions off SIPPs led to all sorts of mad things being planned for a SIPP investment. SIPPs to invest in property, for example, were being set up by estate agents; SIPPs to invest in coins or stamps were being set up by, guess who, coin and stamp dealers; no doubt there were SIPPs in old violins set up by old violin dealers. Which may or may not have been fiddles.

I mentioned that SIPPs were not regulated. And investments like domestic property, coins, racehorses, violins and so on are not regulated either. So you could have had unregulated investments in an unregulated pension arrangement sold by, yes, unregulated sales people – who may also be untrained and are certainly unaccountable. But you can bet your life they would not have been un-paid commission for doing so.

Then, with just four months to go, Flash Gordon stepped in to save the investment universe. In future, all those exotic things would effectively be taxed out of any possible useful existence. And it seems likely now that no dangerous SIPPs will be sold. Hoorah.

But so many people got so excited by how much money they were going to make that they may still be trying to devise cunning ways to sell SIPPs. So for a while yet beware a geek bearing SIPPs.

SIPPs can still be a very useful way to build a up a pension fund that you – not an investment manager – are in charge of. And they will be heavily sold in future. Indeed one pension guru I heard speak recently said that he expected *all* pension plans to have an element of SIPP in them in the future.

A SIPP is simply a sort of pension fund. As mentioned above, it is run by someone called a SIPP trustee on your behalf, who makes sure the law is followed. The advantage is that <u>you</u> decide what your fund is invested in. So if you want to invest in Bolivian mining shares, a REIT (when they exist) in accommodation for Bulgarian grape pickers, or indeed in a FTSE tracker Exchange Traded Fund (see p. 124) you are free to do so. Whatever you choose to invest in, however, you must ask yourself whether it is a good idea.

Traditionally, pension funds are invested in a mixture of shares and bonds. They produce a steady return, so the fund grows (or shrinks when shares go down in value, but hey, it's for the long term and as far as we know they always bounce back). You put in £1,000 a year, the fund earns 7% a year and the managers take out 1.5%, so overall it grows by 5.5% a year. At the end of 30 years, instead of the £30,000 you put in, you have £77,000.

Such a rate of growth may be more or less unrealistic, but you can probably achieve 4.5% without risk by putting the money in a cash account. With charges at zero that would still leave you with £64,750. Now there is not much point in SIPPing this kind of fund (yes, the acronym SIPP has become a noun and well, there isn't a noun that can't be verbed). First because there is not much in there and the SIPP manager's fees, which are normally fixed but could take £500 a year, would actually destroy most of the return. And second, you can get this kind of investment without it being in a SIPP. So what's the point?

HOW TO SIPP

A SIPP is a good idea if you want to be in control of your pension fund and the investments that you are, after all, relying on to grow enough to keep you in retirement. But you also need a certain amount in your fund before it is worth doing, because a SIPP adds another level of charges onto your fund. As well as any charges you pay to buy units in a tracker fund or to buy shares in an Exchange Traded Fund or a REIT (when they begin), the SIPP trustee will charge you an annual fee which could be £500 – though some charge a lot less, others more – just to be your trustee. That fee includes the basic stuff, but if there is anything difficult – like getting assets valued or selling some foreign investments on your behalf – that will be extra. And even junior staff will be charged out at £100 an hour for the time they spend on your behalf. Now if you are paying £100 a month into your pension, £1,200 a year, £500 a year to a SIPP trustee is clearly out of the question. But if you have a big pension fund, say £100,000 or more, and you want it put into a SIPP then £500 a year is just 0.5% of the fund value and you may think it worthwhile. Or indeed you may be able to find it cheaper – £140 a year is about the lowest currently, but prices have fallen and may come down further. On top of these charges any fund you invest your money in will make the same charges it usually does.

One final word of warning on SIPPs. Do remember that any company pension scheme has to let you leave – even if you carry on working for the employer – and let you transfer the value of the pension earned so far into any other approved pension scheme. So you could leave a nice safe guaranteed salary-related pension scheme and move the value of that nice safe guaranteed pension into a risky old SIPP which you use to buy into a REIT which buys holiday flats in the Bulgarian resort of Borgas on the edge of the Black Hole . . . sorry, I mean Sea. Don't do it. Ever. Or even think about it.

LIFESTYLING

Whatever sort of investment you choose for your pension, as you approach the magic time when you fancy a Benefit Crystallisation Event – retirement, as we used to call it – you should consider 'lifestyling'. The problem with investing your pension in stuff like shares is that they are the real manic depressives of the investment world, up one day and down the next for no apparent reason. That's fine if you can wait for the next up. But if you want to retire on a particular day or in a particular year then it can be a real drag.

So many pensions will move your investments out of shares and into something a bit less exciting but a lot more reliable as that fateful day approaches. The word used for this process is 'lifestyling'. I suppose it's as good as any other word that does not convey a nanogram of what it actually means.

Generally, lifestyling is a good thing, so bear it in mind as the years pass.

CHAPTER SEVEN

How Much Can I Save? – What a difference A-Day makes

Since A-Day, 6 April 2006, the rules about how much you can save for your pension have been made much simpler. When you have got to the end of the following 3,000-word explanation of how much you can save you might wonder 'Good God, what were the rules like before?' All I can say is I am really glad I am writing this book now, not a year ago (in fact it was put off for a few months when I made that very point to the publishers).

Simple guide
Q: HOW MUCH CAN I SAVE TOWARDS A PENSION?

A: As much as you like. Or more precisely as much as you earn.

Yes. In a year you can put as much as you earn into a pension fund. As long as that isn't more than £215,000, in which case you can only put in £215,000. And if you earn nothing you can still put in £3,600. So that covers most of us! A minimum of £3,600, a maximum of your earnings. Or £215,000 if you earn more than that.

> **WOMEN AND KIDS**
>
> Anyone can put up to £3,600 a year into a pension, even if they earn nothing. So you can invest in a pension for someone who is nought because of the way the tax relief works (which is explained back on pp. 108–114) you actually put in £2,808 and the taxman puts in £792. And that happens for everyone even if they pay no tax. The good thing

about it as an investment for kids is that it will grow until they are 55 and can take it out. By which time they may just be responsible enough to have all that money of their own! I mention women in the heading because as we saw earlier, women are much less likely to work every adult year God sends than men are. So part of your deal with your bloke could be that if you stay at home and look after the kids, he tops up your pension by up to £3,600 a year (which will only cost him £2,808 or £2,160 if he is a higher-rate tax-payer) and that will help fill the gap in your pension life. Whether he continues to fill a gap in the rest of your life won't matter. The pension will be yours!

The fiddly bits

The upper limits are on the total amount going into the pension. So they include the amount you put in and the amount your employer puts in. So far so simple, if you pay into a money-purchase scheme which saves up your pension money and turns the fund over to you when you reach pension age. You put in 5% of your pay, your employer puts in 10% and that means you can put in another 85% of your pay if you want to. And you can find some way to live without money for a whole year. But it is more complicated if you are in a scheme that promises a pension related to your salary (the different types of pension your employer might offer you are explained in full in Chapter 5). Because although you know how much you put in (actually you probably don't because to most people it is just money they earn but never see, but you can find out from your pay slips – it is typically about 5% of your pay and can range from nothing to 10% or even more), the amount your employer puts in is more obscure. Because whatever they actually put in, they are committed to putting in enough to pay you the pension they have promised. And at the end of the year that promise will be worth more than it was at the start. So the total contribution to your scheme is reckoned to be the extra value of your pension at the end of the year.

OK. Let us suppose that you earn £40,000 – well, you can dream – and that your pension scheme promises you 1/80th of your pay for every year you are in it. So after a year your pension promise has gone up

£40,000/80 = £500. So the extra value of the pension that is promised is £500. And for no reason that I can explain, this amount is then multiplied by ten to give the notional amount that has been contributed to your scheme during the year. That gives £5,000. And that is the amount that is counted as the growth in your fund over the year. As you are allowed to put in up to £40,000 (that's what you earn), you are free to put in another £35,000 into a separate pension scheme if you want . . . and if you can afford to live on nothing for a year.

Incidentally, in case you are wondering, suppose by mistake you did put £36,000 into a pension, putting you £1,000 over the limit: you would have to pay tax of 40% on that £1,000, wiping out the tax advantage of putting it in. Or more than wiping it out for a basic-rate taxpayer. That may seem like punishing the worst off, but really it is to stop the rich and well advised from getting a very low salary and a very high pension contribution.

Now you may be thinking, where am I going to get another £35,000 from anyway? Well, suppose you inherited it. Or won it on the lottery. Or made a big profit selling your house. You could put that money into a pension and get full tax relief on it. Or you could blow it all on a new car. Your choice.

The upper limit of £215,000 will rise each year until 2010/11. After that it will be up to the government of the day to decide what it is. And although it is actually an annual limit, it is called an annual allowance. Don't ask me why, but I suspect 'limit' sounds restrictive while 'allowance' sounds generous.

One more thing on the annual contribution limit. It does not apply in the final tax year before you draw your fund. In that year you can pay in any amount, however huge, that you like. Even if it is more than you earn and more than £215,000. However, tax relief will not be given on any amount above what you earn.

Sorry, I know it's boring, but when I say 'year' I mean the tax year

ANNUAL CONTRIBUTION LIMIT (Officially called 'annual allowance')	
YEAR	AMOUNT
2006/07	£215,000
2007/08	£225,000
2008/09	£235,000
2009/10	£245,000
2010/11	£255,000

which runs from 6 April one year to 5 April the next. So these limits all apply to tax years, not calendar years of January to December. So if you draw your pension in July 2035, that is in the tax year 2034/35 and you can pay as much as you like into your pension in the tax year before that which is 2033/34.

And now you may be thinking this is ridiculous. Not ridiculously complex (you should have seen the old rules) but ridiculously generous. If someone was wealthy, earning say £450,000 a year, they could put in £215,000 into a pension this year and more than that each year of their working life, not to mention £450,000 in the last year – they would have millions in there. All accumulated tax free. In other words at the expense of the rest of us hard-working taxpayers. To deal with that, there is another limit that is imposed – a lifetime limit on how much a pension fund can be worth. In 2006/07 it is fixed at £1.5 million. That amount will also rise year by year as shown in the table. Although it is a lifetime limit it is actually called a lifetime allowance. In fact it is called a Standard Lifetime Allowance because in some circumstances it can be more. See transitional arrangements . . .

Now it doesn't take hard arithmetic to work out that it won't take long, saving up £215,000 a year, to reach the maximum allowed – only seven years if the fund doesn't grow at all. But remember it is not a limit on how much you put in. It is a limit on how much your fund is worth. So if you put in £1 million but investment returns boost that to £2 million by the end of 2010/11, you will be £200,000 over your

LIFETIME PENSION FUND LIMIT	
(officially called: standard lifetime allowance)	
YEAR	AMOUNT
2006/07	£1,500,000
2007/08	£1,600,000
2008/09	£1,650,000
2009/10	£1,750,000
2010/11	£1,800,000

lifetime limit. You are not sent to jail or anything, but you lose the tax relief on the extra. In fact nothing happens at all until you decide to retire. Actually no-one retires any more... a moment comes when you decide to take your retirement benefits. More on this on p. 165.

So. At your retirement you have £200,000 above your lifetime allowance. At that moment, you might think you would have 40% taken off any surplus. After all you have received 40% tax relief on those contributions. But no. You have 55% taken off it. Well actually you have a choice. If the surplus is simply returned to you by cheque, then it is reduced by 55%. If on the other hand you decide to leave it in the fund and to take the extra income It produces then 25% is taken off it.

Here's the arithmetic. First the 25% is just a fine for breaking the rules. It is called a 'Lifetime Allowance Charge' but remember the Lifetime Allowance is in fact a lifetime limit. So the charge is for exceeding that limit. Sounds like a fine to me! Then you can choose. You take the extra as income and it will be taxed as income at 40%. Deduct 25% and then 40% of that and you find that you have lost 55% of the total.

Oh, come on, your arithmetic can't be that bad.

OK, here's a worked example.

Excess	£100,000
Less 25%	£25,000
	£75,000
Less 40%	£30,000
Leaves	£45,000

So you started with £100,000, and you have £45,000 left so the tax man or woman has taken a total of £55,000 from you. The alternative is to take the cash, in which case the 55% is whipped off straight away.

Well I didn't say it was fair, I just said I would explain the arithmetic!

But some of you who have paid attention to the pension deal you have at work will have another question now. What about pension schemes that promise you a pension related to your salary – so-called 'final salary' or 'defined benefit' schemes? Here there is no personal fund, just a promise to pay a pension related to your salary. How do you know what that is worth? The answer is relatively simple. If the pension is not in payment, then you multiply it by 20 (25 if it is being paid) to give the notional capital value of the fund. In other words, if your pension will be £20,000 then you are assumed to have a fund of £20,000 x 20 = £400,000. Well below the limit of £1.5 million. Phew. And it doesn't take much arithmetic to work out that to reach that £1.5 million limit you need a pension of £75,000. So if you earn £112,500 in your last year and your promised pension is two thirds final salary then you will be just at the limit. Anything more and you will be liable to the fine for breaching the lifetime limit.

Of course not everyone will be in this happy position. But the very surprising thing is that it will affect more than 4,000 top civil servants. Anyone in what is called the Senior Civil Service – and there were 4,300 of them on 1 April 2004 – could potentially have earnings at or above this level by the time they reach pension age (which is still 60 for those who joined the Civil Service Pension Scheme before the summer of 2006). So 4,300 top civil servants face a potential reduction in their pension when they retire.

The precise way it will work has yet to be decided. But the trustees of each scheme in the private sector will have to decide how they are to implement the rules. They could do it by offering the member a return of the surplus fund – less the 55% tax charge – or they could pay them the full benefits they were promised but less the extra 25% tax due on the surplus. In the public sector where there is no fund and where there are no trustees then the scheme rules will have to be changed by the Government.

Now, just when you were thinking 'and they call *this* simplification?,' there is another little wrinkle, no – don't be silly – not to iron out, just to be aware of. Generally the new rules from April 2006 apply to people in existing schemes and their pensions. But when it comes to the lifetime limit, there are what are called 'transitional provisions'. In fact there are two different transitional rules. The idea of both is to allow people who have already earned pension benefits which are in excess of the lifetime limit (or may grow to be in excess of it) to protect them.

Welcome to the confusing world of 'primary' and 'enhanced' protection. Most people can happily skip this bit. And those who have sufficient funds to worry about it can afford to – and should – employ a qualified independent financial adviser. But so you know the difficult decisions that face rich people (much better to be poor), here – briefly – is how each works.

Enhanced protection is the better of the two in most circumstances. Whatever the size of your pension pot (and of course I include here the fund you are assumed to have if you are in a salary-related scheme), you can register it for enhanced protection. Whether it is £1 million and you fear that it will exceed the maximum by the time you reach your benefit crystallisation event moment or if it is already £5 million does not matter. By registering it for enhanced protection you put a tight-fitting and impenetrable bag around it which protects it forever from the lifetime allowance tax charge – the fine for exceeding the lifetime limit. And that is not just its value now but whatever its value is when you reach your pension moment. But, and it is a big but ('Does my but look big in this? Gargantuan, my love.' Stephen Fry, 2004), you cannot pay another penny into a pension of any sort. Ever. Full stop. And if you are in a salary-related scheme you cannot earn any more pension rights. Each year that passes you will not earn more 1/60ths or whatever. Your 1/60ths cannot be turned into 1/50ths or 1/40ths. And if you have a pay rise then the 1/60ths you have earned so far will not apply to the higher pay. Well sort of almost in the last case. Your pay can rise by up to a maximum of 5% a year (or with the rise in prices if that is higher). But any promotion or extras above that cannot count for your pension.

So in effect you withdraw from pensions, apart from the humungous pot you already have, and say 'I'm not playing after 6 April 2006 so I don't care what the rules are, na na nana na'.

You can register for enhanced protection up to 6 April 2009. But – another big but is arriving – you must not pay into a pension of any sort after 6 April 2006. If you have, even £1, you have already lost the right to enhanced protection.

That is enhanced protection. Its cousin, primary protection, is more complicated, requires a bit of arithmetic and is generally not so much use. To get primary protection you have to have a pension pot of more than £1.5 million at 6 April 2006, or rights to a final salary pension of more than £75,000 at that date. Suppose you have £2 million, or you have already an entitlement to a salary-related pension of £100,000 a year. That is one third more than the limit. You can register that pension value at 6 April 2006 and then you will always be able to have a pension worth one and a third times the limit, whatever that is when you reach your pension moment. So if that is in five years when the limit is £1.8 million, you will be able to have £1,800,000 × 1.3333 = £2,400,000. Anything above that will be subject to the charge. The last day to register for primary protection is 5 April 2009

SMALL POTS
We move now from the gargantuan to the minuscule. New rules allow people who have had the foresight – or lack of – to save up very

little for their pension, to cash their pension fund in. In other words, forget about converting it to an income for life and just get it back. Less some tax of course. To do this, your total pension funds have to be worth £15,000 or less, and you have to be aged at least 60.

The limit is actually set at 1% of the lifetime limit. So it is £15,000 in 2006/07 and will rise as that rises, reaching £18,000 by 2010/11. Pension funds below this limit are called 'trivial'. Now before you flounce out in a huff, having a trivial pension fund is quite useful.

When you cash your trivial fund in you can keep a quarter of it as tax-free cash. The rest is taxed as if it was part of your earned income for the tax year. So if it takes you over the limit for higher-rate tax then some or all of it will be taxed at 40%. So it is worth picking carefully the year you claim it. Make sure the payment falls in the tax year when your income is likely to be lower and the tax charged is thus reduced.

If you are a member of a company pension scheme that has a set pension age higher than 60, you can still take your trivial pension fund in cash at age 60 if you want. If it is a salary-related scheme then the value is 20 times the pension due (or 25 times a pension already being paid). So your pension has to be £750 a year or less in 2006/07 or £600 if it is already being paid.

But. (There is always a but in pension rules – in fact that itself is a rule:

> ### Rule of obscurity
>
> ### There is always a 'but' in pension rules.

and it is usually a bummer.) But, it is your *total* pension value that has to be less than £15,000. So if you have a pension from your job and a personal pension, they have to be added together. Similarly you cannot cash in one fund worth £10,000 if you have another worth

£12,000. The total has to be less than the limit and you have to cash them in at the same time.

But there is a loophole here. Once you have cashed in your pension fund, there is nothing to stop you paying into another one from 60 right up to 75 as long as you have earnings up to that age. You cannot do the trick twice and cash in a further fund! But it is worth looking at your fund at 60 to see if it is small enough to cash in. Because you can just recycle the money back into another pension if you want.

Here is the arithmetic. The pension fund is £15,000 and you can take a quarter tax-free which is £3,750. That leaves £11,250 which is taxed at 22%, leaving you with £8,775 added to the tax free £3,750 so you actually get £12,525. As long as you have earned that much in the tax year, you can then put that straight back into a pension and get full tax relief on all of it. So you put in £12,525 and the taxman adds £3,532.69 to make a total of £16,057.69 in your pension. So overnight your 'trivial' pension pot has grown by more than £1,000! And if you are a higher-rate taxpayer the arithmetic is even kinder and you end up with £17,500 in your pension. An overnight gain of £2,500. Suddenly your pension pot is slightly less trivial.

The downside is it has to stay there and provide some sort of pension for you. You cannot wait for it to get trivial again and repeat the exercise. Though as it is a new pension you can take 25% of it in cash at some point tax free.

CHAPTER EIGHT

Debt and Houses: And other fun stuff

Saving for a pension is generally considered a GOOD THING. If you go into a room full of financial advisers, actuaries, insurance industry bosses and personal finance journalists and say 'saving for a pension is not a good idea', you would pretty soon be shouted down. Probably even quicker than you would run a mile when you realised who was in there.

But in fact it is not always a good thing. Far from it. The best advice normally is that if you have spare money, the first thing you should do with it – ignoring the stuff you would prefer to use it for like shopping or holidays – is not to save it or invest it but use it to pay off your debts.

The arithmetic is simple (no really, it is this time). If you borrow £1,000 you are going to be paying the lender at least £70 a year and sometimes £300 a year for the fun of doing it. Say the average is £150. If you give the same bank £1,000 to save for you then you will be lucky to get £50 back at the end of the year, and that's before you pay the Chancellor £10 tax. So there is little point in having a debt of £1,000 and savings of £1,000 (except of course for the bank). You pay £150 on one and get back £40 on the other. Net loss £110 a year. But if you use the £1,000 saved up to pay off the £1,000 of debt, you are £110 a year better off. Enough for a small trip to the shops or a very short holiday. Bognor's very nice at this time of year, I believe.

Shakespeare said, or rather he got Polonius to say in *Hamlet*, 'Neither a borrower nor a lender be'. He really hated the financial services industry, that Will. Because their whole business depends on us being one or the other and preferably both. And many of us are both. We borrow from the bank at 15% on our credit card and lend to the same bank – they call it saving – at 4%. And then we wonder why between them they made more than £30 billion profit in 2004/05.

So no surprise that we are more than a trillion pounds in debt. Or at least half of us are, because around half the households in the country have no debt at all. And before you say 'creeps,' think about it. Someone has to lend you the money you borrow! It's what the mathematicians call a zero sum game. What they mean by that is that the banks win the game and the sum in your account is always zero or less. Anyway, rule number 1 is if you can't obey Polonius, then don't be a borrower AND a lender. Use spare cash to pay off debt.

Now when debt is on a credit card at 15.9% or a personal loan at 6.9% or an overdraft at 27.5% and your spare money is in an ISA or a current account or even invested in unit trusts, then rule number 1 makes excellent sense. If you have ever been advised to save or invest when you had debt, sack that adviser now. And then consider a formal complaint and compensation.

'But are not pensions different?' I hear you ask, rather properly. 'I have a debt on my credit card but I still think it makes sense to save for the long-term future in my pension.'

Well, you've put your but in and here now is my big but barging into the book: I am going to have a word about debt. If you have none then feel free to read this section anyway and feel smug. If you do have debt, do not feel free to skip it.

I mentioned that we have more than a trillion pounds of debt. It is actually around £1.2 trillion. And in case 'trillion' makes it sound quite small, let me write it out for you – £1,200,000,000,000. A trillion is a million times a million. I don't know about you but I cannot imagine really what a million pounds actually looks like. But if I could, I would then have to imagine a million of those millions. Nope. It's too much.

Most of that trillion is mortgages. In fact mortgages are about a trillion all by themselves. Leaving about £200 billion – £200,000,000,000 – in true personal debt owed on credit cards, bank loans, hire purchase, overdrafts and those brilliant offers on daytime TV. And that money is owed by just under half the population. Bank of England research says around 45% of families have debt and 55% do not. It says all sorts of other weird things too so we do not really know if the average debt – for those who have it – is £4,500, £9,800 or £15,000 each. But whatever it is, it is a lot.

Now I am not against debt. It is a useful way to balance a regular income with fluctuating demand. But if you spend more than you earn year after year, you will get into trouble. Period. As Americans used to say. Or, as people say now, end of. So while you are thinking about putting money into a pension (and you have got three-quarters the way through a book about just that, so don't pretend you're not!), you should spend a few minutes sorting out your other finances. If you do you will have more spare money and you can then (a) put more into the pension you finally decide on or (b) put the same in and use the extra money to do nice stuff.

CUTTING DEBT

This can only be a brief guide because this book is about pensions not debt. Step 1 is to write down all your debts and the rate of interest on them. You probably won't know what it is but your credit card statement should tell you, and if it doesn't then you can call the card helpline – which the statement will tell you – and find out. Write it down. Ditto other debts.

Then you have to draw up a plan to start paying off the debt, with the highest interest rate first. If it is a credit card then you can simply increase your monthly payment. At the moment if you do not pay it off in full (and I know you don't or you wouldn't be counting it as a debt) you pay the 'minimum'. This amount is fixed by the credit card company to make your debt stretch into the dim and distant future. Let me ask you a simple question. You owe £1,000 on your credit card and the rate of interest you pay is a modest 15.9% APR. If you pay off the minimum used by most cards – 2% of the debt or £5 if that is more – how long will it be before the debt is paid off in full?

(a) **Two years**
(b) **Five years**
(c) **Eight years three months**
(d) **More than 20 years**

In fact it is (d). A staggering 21 years three months. Thank you Lloyds TSB Gold card. But many others are as bad or even worse.

So the answer is not to pay the minimum. The trick they use is to let you pay a percentage of the debt. So in month one you pay £20.25 off. That reduces the debt and next month you pay £20.09. A year later the payment has fallen to £18.42. And it is only by November 2020 that it has fallen to the fixed fiver where it stays. The least painful way to deal with this is to look at your current payment – say it is £20.25 a month – and take out a standing order for that much, so you pay off a fixed amount. After all if you can afford it now, you can afford it for the next six years and five months to repay the debt in full. That way you end up paying £562 in interest, whereas paying the minimum you end up paying £1,332 in interest – more than you borrowed in the first place!

You may of course look horrified at a debt of £1,000 still lasting for more than six years. Even after you have made that effort to pay it off. After all £1,000 on a credit card doesn't really sound that very much does it? Fine. Double your repayment to £40.50 and it will take you just two years six months. That's more like it. When the most expensive debt is paid off (by the way, cut up your card and do not spend any more on it), pay off the next and so on. Soon you will have a debt-free you and loads more money to spend. Or to put into your pension.

BORROWING

I know I said do not borrow any more. But sometimes, well, people being people, it just happens doesn't it? A bit like sex with someone you never intended. (Of course borrowing isn't as nice as sex. But it's a mistake that lasts a lot longer and costs a great deal more. I'm assuming it was safe sex of course. I'll stop this thought here.) So this short section is about safe borrowing.

First, keep your eye on your current account. If you are going overdrawn regularly, make sure that it is approved overdrawing. Some banks will offer you this at just 8% or even less. Others charge two or even three times that. But all charge far more if it is unauthorised borrowing. And before you complain about these extortionate charges for an overdraft the bank hasn't agreed to, think what it is. You are taking the bank's money without permission. Theft some might call it. Indeed in France they do. It is a crime.

Second, if you really want a credit card, make use of the many good deals on offer. Of course some are offering 0% on spending or on balance transfers. Now they require a lot of self discipline (don't knock self discipline. It's saving money for someone you love). But if you have a debt already, you can take out a balance transfer card and move it to that and then try to pay it off while the deal lasts. The 0% normally lasts at least six months and some last up to a year. But beware, some of them charge you 2% on the money transferred – avoid them. Alternatively, you can pay off the debt in a disciplined way (see above) and use the 0% card just for purchases. But draw up a routine to repay the items before the 0% runs out.

The alternative is to find a really cheap card. Some will let you move a balance and pay a low rate for the life of the balance. In other words until it is paid off. So if your card charges say 15.9%, you may move the balance to one that charges 6.9% (the current best buy on life-of-balance transfers). That makes the debt cost much less. And if you do want a card to spend with (in other words, you need to spend more than your income ... mmm) then you can get a card with a low interest rate on purchases. But there is of course a Golden Rule of Prosperity about borrowing.

> **Rule of Prosperity**
>
> **Never borrow for longer than the thing you bought will last.**

So if you use the card to pay for a holiday for instance, make sure the debt is gone by the time you want another – and if it's not, don't go! If you pay for Christmas, make sure you repay that debt in a year.

Third, never ever ever consider taking on a consolidation loan. Borrowing money to pay off debt is not paying off debt. It is taking on more and always at worse terms. Do not believe the adverts that say the terms are not worse. They always are or they would not be in business.

So if you have debt, start a plan to pay it off. And do that before you even consider saving or investing.

Now. I am going to contradict that advice and – because I am a pretty special kind of writer – I am going to contradict it twice. In different ways.

First, I am going to tell you a story. It is called 'The Time I Ignored My Own Advice – and Why.'

When I was first in business, I used to have a current account with an overdraft facility of £5,000 and a savings account. Into my savings account I put a fixed percentage of every penny that came in so that I knew I could pay my VAT and my income tax. And it sat there waiting for those moments each quarter and half-year when I had to steel myself to write what seemed to me then a Very Large Cheque to HM Revenue & Customs. And it sat there in cash earning some pathetic rate of interest, even if I was using my overdraft facility and paying the bank an extortionate rate of interest on that. But the net cost between the two was never more than a couple of hundred pounds a year or so. And I called it my 'sleep at night' cost. The arithmetical argument to use my tax money to pay off my overdraft was compelling. But the psychological argument to keep a positive pot and a negative pot of money was overwhelming. The negative pot didn't cost me that much. And the positive pot made sure that when the horrible tax bill came, I knew I had enough to pay it. So the small amount it cost me in the year was money very well spent. Illogical though it may be, captain, it was human.

Now, as promised, I am going to contradict the general advice in a second and, again as promised, different way. And incidentally answer your question about whether pensions are different from other sorts of investment. *Vis à vis* paying off debt that is.

When it comes to pensions the arithmetic is not always as much against you as it is with others sorts of investment. First, the taxperson puts in 28p for every pound you put in (67p if you are a higher-rate taxpayer). Second, if you are in a company scheme then for every pound you put in your boss should put in the same at least. So for £1 spent there is £2.28 in your pension. And if you are in a salary-related scheme your boss probably commits to putting in at least twice what you put in. Which means about £3.28. Or £3.67 if you are a higher-rate taxpayer. So your money generates a big return before it earns a penny in interest. Third, the money is there for the long term and the return it earns will itself earn money next year. Compound interest weaves its magic. So a pound you do not invest now will mean a big hole – about £14 – in your fund in 30 years' time. So I am not going to say pay off every penny of debt before you invest in a pension. But please start paying off that debt. The 55% of households without debt are a lot happier than the 45% with it, a survey shows. Actually I made that up. But you know it is true.

SHOULD I BUY A HOUSE?

Yes. But instead of investing in a pension? Yes. And here is why. A house you rent is only yours as long as your income is high enough to pay the rent. And nowadays rent can be reviewed every 12 months.

What you can afford on a salary will be very different from what you can afford on even a good pension. But a house you have bought is yours. And yes, it may end up too big for your frail 85-year-old body. And yes, the pittance you live on without a pension may mean that getting the roof fixed or the boiler changed or the lounge recarpeted becomes impossible. Never mind. These are better problems to have than homelessness.

By now of course you realise that your house cannot *be* your pension – see pp. 26 – but it can be your home. And that is priority number one. It's what a home is for – to live in, not to act as an investment or a source of future funding. It's guaranteed shelter. And until you have to do without it, you do not realise how important that is to your welfare and happiness.

And those rules about paying off debt before you invest do not apply to the debt of your mortgage – for two reasons. First, the interest rate you pay is normally very low. Lower in some cases than the return you can get on some investments. Second, it is a loan which is for an asset that not only holds its value but chances are will be worth more in five years than it is now. Try selling that suit you bought. Or those CDs you put on your 15.9% credit card. Or of course that anniversary meal you ate or that holiday you enjoyed. Sort your home out and then think about the pension.

Before we leave the house stuff, remember that it is your biggest expense. And therefore offers the biggest scope for saving money. So just as I had a little diversion for sorting out debt – and go back and read that now if you skipped it – we are going to have a tiny detour round not wasting money on your home. You may have ignored some of this advice before. Don't do that again please. Or you may get revision.

How much is your mortgage? Let's say it is £100,000. OK yours may be more or less than that, but converting the examples below to your circumstances is much easier if we start with £100,000 and it is not far from the average mortgage in the UK. Suppose you have a bog standard variable rate mortgage. And before you say 'oh no we got a great deal' remember that great deals run out and tip you into the standard variable rate (often sanitised to SVR, but that lays it open to a backronym – Scandalous Valueless Rip-off). Now the SVR as I write is around 6.5%. If you have a repayment mortgage of £100,000 over 25 years, that will be costing you £675 a month or £8,102 a year. Now you can easily get that cut to 4.5% by remortgaging. That will cost you £556 a month or £6,670 a year. A saving of £1,432 a year. Making the change will cost you a few hundred pounds in fees of various sorts – though check out the deals that pay some or even all of these for you – but the deal should last five years. So it is a big saving for a few phone calls and a couple of hours' work. By the time you read this the SVR may be lower (or of course higher), but the margin between it and good deals you can easily get is always around 2%. So the arithmetic still works.

Now you may have been scratching your head over the last paragraph. 'I don't know where this bloke gets his figures from. Our mortgage is almost exactly £100,000 and we pay far less than that. So I guess we don't have the SVR thingy. So we're OK. But I thought it was around 6% or something. Oh well I'll look it up tomorrow.'

Actually the key word in all that above was 'repayment'. Is your mortgage a repayment one? Or an interest only one? It's a pretty vital difference, because at the end of the 25 years with the repayment mortgage you will owe nothing – the house (and all that security in old age stuff I mentioned) is yours. With an interest only mortgage you will have paid the lender £162,500 over the 25 years but at the end you will still owe the £100,000 you borrowed. It is interest only. You just pay the interest. The debt, the amount you borrowed is not paid off. Now of course these loans are cheaper as you go along. In fact a loan of £100,000 will cost you £6,500 a year (£100,000 × 6.5%) rather than £8,102. *But the house is never yours*. So if you have an interest only loan (and one in seven new loans are interest only, with no clear investment plan to repay it), sort that out. And I don't mean reckoning that by the time 25 years have past at least one distant relative will have left you something. First, only one in two people have any expectation of being left anything. And if you are left something it is more likely to be a few thousand pounds than a few hundred thousands. In fact put a bookmark in here, stop reading and sort it out now. Not many things are more important than reading this book, but that is one.

INSURANCE

And while we are on the subject of saving money – insurance. I am not the world's biggest fan of insurance. By which I mean I treat it with disdain at best and distrust at worst. Most of it is unnecessary. And the more expensive it is the less it is needed. So getting rid of unnecessary insurance is a good way to save money that you can then put to good use in a pension.

One way profits on loans and mortgages are boosted is to add on what is called payment protection insurance or PPI (aka Punitively Priced Imposition). This is supposed to take over your loan repayments if you have an accident or fall ill or are made redundant. It is hugely profitable for the companies who sell it because very few people claim, and of those that do around one in seven is turned down. The Financial Services Authority has expressed concern about the way PPI is sold and its suitability for many clients. It is currently under investigation by the Office of Fair Trading. If you have it on a credit card, note that it will only make the minimum payments each month and may only pay up for a year. It is best cancelled. On a loan you will have paid for it upfront in most cases and cancelling it is harder. But it is best avoided in future. Most jobs come with sick pay for up to six months.

Other forms of add-on insurance for things such as lost credit cards, extended warranties and ID theft are never worth having. Critical illness insurance is very expensive and a waste of money. Use permanent health insurance instead if it helps you sleep at night. But check how much time on full and half pay your employer will give you. And if you are considering private health insurance – don't. Much better to save the premiums up in an account and use that if you need to pay for health care.

Even life assurance is oversold. If you are in a salary-related pension scheme you will get an in-service death benefit of three or four times your pay. Many other deals come with life assurance built in. If you have dependants, think what they may need and pay for that. And remember to cancel it when they cease being dependent.

I've probably saved you a couple of thousand a year already. Why not put half into a pension and the other half into a nice pair of shoes?

BUY TO LET

This isn't a book about buying property to let it out, but a brief word here is probably the right place. Like shares property brings in regular income – from the rent – and shows a capital gain, giving you two ways to win. And domestic property – houses, flats, bungalows and so on – has shown the most consistent growth and the least down-time of any investment. In my view, supply (limited) and demand (growing) mean that it will continue to be the best place to invest money.

So why don't more of us do it? One answer, of course, is that if you have a map showing Treasure Island you don't go to a crowded street and shout 'Hey, look! I've got a map with all the loot on it!' First, you'll probably be taken away by security guards; second, if you're not, then by the time you get there the treasure will be gone. Basically, the really rich folk keep quiet about just how good property investments are. Consistent, generation-proof wealth has been created more through property than anything else – just look at the four families who own the centre of London if you don't believe me. Where do you think the phrase 'safe as houses' came from? Eighteenth century property development.

The other reason more of us don't do it is that it's difficult. You can't buy shares in domestic property, so you cannot invest £100 a month or even a £10,000 lump sum: you need capital. (REITs will help eventually, and you'll be able to be put them into a pension.)

The other way of doing it is to borrow the money, buy the property and let it out. This *can* work . . . but only with the right property in the right place at the right time. I once met a couple , both teachers, who had done just that in Greenwich, South London, just before property prices there took off with the Docklands light railway and so on. They made a fortune and gave up work, but generally it's not so easy. And it has to be done as an *alternative* to a formal pension plan.

If you still feel you want to do it, here's a quick guide:

1. Location, location, location. Choose somewhere with a transient and well paid population. Young professionals are ideal, heading for that first job and restless for the next. Think about cities with headquarters, university towns, places near financial services companies – that sort of thing.

2. Find a mortgage. There is a huge choice now in what are called buy-to-let mortgages. You need one of those because residential mortgages do not let you rent out the property. Normally, buy-to-let is an interest-only mortgage so you repay the capital when you sell the property in the future. That makes it cheaper ... but riskier. There are three extra costs with buy-to-let mortgages. First, you can only borrow around 80% of the purchase price, though some will go a bit higher, so you need a hefty deposit. Second, interest rates are slightly higher than the best you can get for buying a home you will live in. But competition is fierce and you can find reasonable rates. Fixed rate is often preferred because the rent is fixed and the profit is clear. But make sure you know the length of the fixed rate and what happens after that – what rate will it go to and what are the penalties if you switch to another lender. The lender will insist that the property can be rented out for around 125 or 130 per cent of the mortgage payments. And when they do that calculation they may ignore the discount on the mortgage. So a £100,000 property will have to bring in a rent of around £700 a month. It will help you sleep at night if the ratio is more like 130% to 150%.

   Make sure the mortgage is flexible – in other words you can pay more or less each month if you want. With buy-to-let it is a good idea to make sure you can miss a payment occasionally when the property is empty and no rent is coming in. The average void as they call it is four weeks a year. Always try to pay more in subsequent months – or in advance – to make up the difference.

Third, there will be fees to pay to the lender and commission to pay to the mortgage broker who arranges the mortgage – many buy-to-let deals are only available through brokers. That fee can be as high as 0.5 per cent of the advance – so £500 on a £100,000 loan. But a broker can often find you a better deal than you could get yourself.

3. Get a good managing agent. They will do all the hard work of finding and vetting tenants, drawing up contracts, collecting the rent, preparing an inventory, inspecting the property, dealing with problems at the beginning, middle and end of the contract. They will also hold the deposit – between one and two months' rent.

4. Set aside money for furnishing the property. Even 'unfurnished' lettings may need decorating and you will have to provide carpets, curtains, light bulbs and a fully-equipped kitchen and bathroom. Any fitted gas appliances, such as fires and boilers, will have to comply with stringent safety regulations and electrical fittings and appliances will have to be properly installed and safe. Both will have to be tested for safety each year. Smoke and carbon monoxide detectors are a good idea. If you decide to furnish the property, you must make sure that all soft furnishings comply with modern safety standards.

5. Don't forget the cost of the inevitable repairs, renewals, decorations, and cleaning between tenants. A good-looking home will be let more quickly, and it is very important to keep the home occupied. Too many blank months – 'voids' is the jargon – and you will find the year's profit disappearing very rapidly.

Nowadays lettings are for a period of six months and can be terminated by either side at that date, so there should be no fears about getting rid of tenants. Awkward customers can, however, stretch this period out and leave you with no income and nowhere to let to anyone else.

Buying to let is more like trading than investing – you have to buy the capital asset and pay the expenses of running it and collecting the income. But professionals in the field estimate that you can make a return of 10 per cent a year – more in some areas and on some types of property. Of course, you can make less or even lose money, so it's important that you take care of all the details first. Remember too that it's a long-term investment – ideal for your pension – but also a long-term commitment.

You can get help from a local residential letting agent, and you can find them in most High Streets; some are also regular estate agents that sell property. Many of them belong to the Association of Residential Letting Agents (ARLA), which ensures its members are competent to manage rented property. Most important, they can give you advice about the local market – what kind of property is in demand, and what kind is not. Most do not charge for advice, but they will charge if you use their services.

No investment is completely free of risk, but buying to let *can* be profitable and there is nothing like walking down the street past a house, which you don't live in, and which you know is yours.

One big word of warning. Selling property as an investment is **unregulated**. That's the big word. Loads of estate agents and wide boys were gearing up for a bonanza when it seemed that bricks and mortar (if only: chipboard and sprayed cement in many cases) could be put in a SIPP (see p. 131). They now have lots of ideas and little to do with them. So expect a lot of schemes to sell you sure-fire investments in the property world that they cannot call a pension but they imply is a great long-term investment. Most of them won't be, however, so be very careful about buy-to-let if you don't do all the choosing yourself.

UNREGULATED STUFF

While you're thinking about alternatives to a pension that are not regulated, your mind might be turning to other things that were being touted as good investments for an imaginative SIPP – things like gold bars, coins, stamps, antique furniture. They are all unregulated too. You're bored with having £10,000 in a cash ISA earning less than 5% a year. That's never going to produce enough to keep you in the lap of luxury at 60, so you want to spread out. After all, isn't diversification the thing? And what was that risk reward stuff you read about earlier?

If you think the charges for ordinary old investments are high – up to around 5% up front and then up to 1.5% to 2.5% a year of the value – then the charges for buying and selling other things are eye watering. You know how when you buy a new car, they say you drive it off the forecourt and straight back on and it has cost you £5,000? Why? Because if you tried to sell it back, that £15,000 brand-new car would now be worth £10k as a used or at least pre-owned vehicle. It's much the same with all that antique stuff. Take auctions. In some ways, an auction is the ideal place to buy and sell antiques, wine, pictures and so on. It is a perfect market, and nowadays a global one, as people can see what's on sale and bid live from all over the world. So you arrange with your SIPP trustee that you have the authority to go along to a sale and buy ... errr ... Royal Doulton Bunnykins figures. Now don't laugh. I mention this because at the height of the SIPPs excitement I got this press release. 'Bunnykins Recommended for New SIPPs Pension Schemes'. It goes on, 'Bunnykins, the family of figurines created by Royal Doulton, could be among the best investments for anyone looking to set up a new SIPPs pension scheme ... Many Bunnykins figurines have appreciated massively in value during the past 30 years and could be a great asset for SIPPs investors.' Now that may be right or wrong. I am not – and never have been, Senator McCarthy – a Royal Doulton Bunnykins collector, still less an expert in them as an investment vehicle.

But I do know this. Physical objects – coins, wine, cars, furniture,

Bunnykins figures – are *not* covered by any rules governing investments, even when they are sold as investments. So that press release can happily say 'certain models have risen ten times in value, from just a few pounds to several hundreds of pounds, in the past decade' without having to justify it, explain the strange arithmetic (several hundred divided by a few is not ten), or tell you that other Bunnykins figures have not done that, that the price of Bunnykins figures can go down as well as up and that there is no future guarantee of the demand for or price of Bunnykins figures.

But suppose you read this and think a few Bunnykins figures will be a fun way to invest for your future outside a pension scheme. You buy all three books about collecting them and mug up. You discover that some are coming up for sale at the London auction house Hammer & Co and you think you will invest a small amount in Bunnykins.

You buy the catalogue and mark down the Bunnykins figures you like the look of which means (although they are all so cute) to you, as a hard-headed investor, that the estimate looks good compared with the price of the figures on the market. You register with the desk and get your number – 383 – which by a massive coincidence is the number of the house you lived in when you met your true love. You hope that is a lucky omen. At the sale you bid on them and are thrilled to find that they go for what you think are good prices – not much above the estimates. In fact, you buy quite a collection and by the end of the sale you have 15 lots – a real display cabinet full! You carefully add up all your bids and the total is £5,000. According to the Royal Doulton Bunnykins Standard Catalogue 3rd edition you bought on eBay they are worth a fair bit more than that. How easy is this?

You ask someone what happens now and they show you where to pay. It looks like a bank with glass screens and a big queue. Finally, it's your turn. You show your number 383 (it makes you smile again; perhaps it did bring you good luck), give your name and they print out your bill. For £6,175. 'Sorry, there seems to be something wrong? I added up the lots they came to £5,000.'

Everyone is so polite at London auction houses. The cashier looks at you and explains patiently that there is a buyer's premium charged on top of the price you bid, the 'hammer price' as they call it, and she refers you to the catalogue where the premium is set out. It is 20%, a fifth more on top of what you bid. But hang on a minute, 20% of £5,000 is £1,000, not £1,175. As the words form on your lips, you see that the bill has £1,000 and under it £175, accompanied by the dreaded acronym VAT. Not on the hammer price – antiques are generally free of VAT – but on the premium. With VAT you are, in fact, paying a premium which adds 23.5% to the price you actually bid. OK, for lots over £100,000 that comes down a bit. But not for five grand's worth of Bunnykins figures. You hand over your credit card, having a vague thought that will help you to complain later if you change your mind. 'You're aware we make a 2% surcharge on credit card payments?' the cashier says, voice rising into a question at the end. That would be another £123.50! Er, no. 'Do you have a debit card?' You do. And you are pretty sure there is enough money in it – just. You hand it over and wonder if you will go overdrawn before you can transfer the money from your other savings account. You smile when you think that money is only earning you 4.5% a year.

On the journey home, you worry about the price. And those worries are echoed by your beloved – why are beloveds always so sensible and why is that always manifested *after* you have done something worrying? – and confirmed when you make a couple of calls to dealers and find problems getting an offer even close to what you paid for the figures. So, with a tingling feeling at the back of your neck, you realise you may have made a mistake. You decide you are not really sure that Bunnykins figures are the best way to save for your retirement. Next day it's back to Hammer's. They politely tell you that they cannot refund any money but they will put them in the next sale of Royal Doulton – in four months – if that is what you want. It is.

Four months on and at the sale some of your figures go for slightly less than you paid, some slightly more but when you add up the prices bid, to your immense relief, your 15 figures fetch a total of £5,000!

Phew. You await your cheque. Three weeks later, it arrives. For £4,118.75. Because guess what? They have charged you 15% commission on each lot. And yes VAT is added to that. Total deductions £881.25. So you have just lost £2,056.25. You really wish you had kept the money in your cash ISA.

The difference between the selling price and buying price exists, of course, in all businesses. They would not be in business long if it didn't. It is called the turn, the profit or the margin. But in the antique and collectibles business it is anything but marginal. By buying and immediately selling your £5,000 figures, you have lost a third of your money. You can see why the 'hammer price' is known in the trade as 'the price no buyer pays and no seller receives'. And high as these charges are, dealers with shop fronts will make an even bigger turn because they have to keep stock, perhaps for months, before they sell it, paying rent and staff meanwhile. So when you see a coin or a stamp priced in a catalogue, expect to get about half that if you are selling – after you have argued about whether the condition is 'fine' or just 'good'.

There is another important lesson here. If you are going to invest in movable stuff, remember that it has to grow in value a hell of a lot before you have even paid the buying and selling charges. In order simply to get your money back, your Bunnykins figures would have to have increased in value by 50%, selling at a hammer price of £7,500. Then you would get a cheque from Messrs Hammer, Block, and Tackle (founded 1742) for £6,178.13, a profit of just £3.13. But at least you would have had the pleasure of saying to friends 'Have I shown you my collection of rare Bunnykins figures?' 'How sweet.' 'Yes, aren't they pretty? And do you know they are also a very sound investment.' 'No!' 'Yes really. In fact, they're my pension.' 'Ah, fancy.'

Stick with financial services products. They are cheaper. Usually safer. And regulated.

CHAPTER NINE

The Longest Holiday: 20 years' unpaid leave

Or maybe it will be 30. Because as we see in Chapter 3, Live Long and Prosper?, some estimates already suggest that at 60 we can expect 30 years of life. And even at 65 a big proportion of us will survive until we are 95. My view is that we should all retire later and that means working longer. In other words we share out the extra life we are going to have – some working, some holiday. We cannot really expect to have all that extra life as paid leave. That's what this chapter is about – when to retire?

COMPANY SCHEMES

If you have a salary-related pension, especially one paid for by tax-payers, then you can just sit back and look forward to this long paid vacation. Probably. There is a doomsday scenario which sees a future government faced with a serious financial crisis, which decides to cut back on the growing and unfunded commitments to people who have been employed in the public sector. Especially those due to people who have not yet retired. When the Government decided to keep pension age at 60 for existing public sector employees, many commentators said at the time the deal was unsustainable and could be changed by a future government. Less likely is that it will cut back on pensions already in payment to people who have retired. But who knows what the world will be like by 2050? I certainly won't.

If you have a salary-related pension from a private company, then I would sit up rather than sit back and definitely keep your eyes open.

The company could go bust (even be sent over the edge by pension commitments, as US firms Polaroid and Bethlehem Steel were) or could decide to wind up its pension scheme. In either case the pensions paid to existing employees have first call on the money, but if there is not enough and if the demands on the Pension Protection Fund (see p. 88) are sufficient, then those benefits may be at risk. And if you have not retired then the company may join the growing number whose pension funds are frozen and where future contributions to the scheme are not allowed.

If you are part of a company scheme, you have to follow the rules about when you can draw your pension. About one in two people in occupational pension schemes can draw their pension at 60. A few fix a lower age, about a quarter fix an age between 61–64 and about a quarter fix 65. This age is separate from the age you stop work. New laws begin on 1 October 2006 which ban all aspects of age discrimination at work. Although employers will still be able to fix a retirement age for staff, it must be 65 or older. So most employees in a company pension scheme will be able to draw their pension before they have to stop work. Schemes may raise the pension age to match the legal minimum requirement age, though such moves will be unpopular. Another big change from A-Day allows people to draw their pension *and* carry on working for the same company – prior to A-Day you could not do that. But although the law will allow it, the rules of many schemes will not. Where they do, people could draw a full pension at 60 and work on until they are 65.

If you pay into AVCs or a stakeholder scheme that your employer contributes to, then you may have to draw those benefits at the same age you draw your company pension.

If you have any other sort of pension, then you have a pension fund. Remember the little pot with your name on it? Now is the time to decide what to do with it. And that is what this chapter is about.

PICK YOUR AGE

Under the A-Day changes, no-one retires. The word 'retire' and 'retirement' have gone from the law. Instead we have the catchy phrase 'Benefit Crystallisation Event' or, of course, BCE. Until April 2010 you can declare a BCE at any age from 50 to 75. After that the lower age is raised to 55. Whoomph. Just like that. So if you are born on 31 March 1960 or the years before that, remember that if you do not declare a BCE before 1 April 2010 you will have to wait until you are 55. If you were born on 1 April 1960 or later, then your minimum age for a BCE will be 55.

Having written a whole paragraph using the phrase BCE I am beginning to feel how stupid it is. I really think 6 April 2006 should be called TLA-Day rather than A-Day. The problem is that under the new rules you can retire more than once, and that even if you retire you do not have to stop work or change jobs. Working is unrelated to getting your pension or, as the civil servants would like you to call it, 'crystallising your benefits'. And the moment you decide to do that is of course a Benefit Crystallisation Event. So 'retire' has become ex-dictionary. But it is so silly, and you are such sensible readers, I will use the word 'retirement' as shorthand for 'BCE' (OK I know it's longer!) and 'retire' for declaring one. I will put a few BCEs in just to remind you of the real world.

If you have your own pension fund – even if you also pay into a company scheme – you can pick when you retire. Here comes the but – see earlier note about AVCs and a fund your employer paid into as well. And because we are all living longer and longer, the younger you choose to turn your fund into a pension the less you will get.

While you are paying in, your fund is growing growing growing and then there is a moment when you want to stop work, stop paying in and convert that fund into an annual income – a pension. At least that's how it used to be. Since A-Day the choices have become a lot more complex. The pension you buy with your fund is called an annuity. Don't ask why, it just is. And be grateful it is not called an LCB – Lifetime Crystallised Benefit. Come to think of it. . . .

With an annuity you give the insurer the whole of your fund (after taking out your 25% tax free because that is almost always a good idea for reasons I explain later). In exchange the insurance company promises to give you an income for life. In theory that income should return all of the fund to you over your life and give you the money your declining fund is still earning.

It is a classic insurance company gamble. If you die younger than expected the insurance company keeps any of the fund that is left, so it is quids in. If you live a lot longer than expected, the income it gives you over those years is worth more than the fund and you win the bet. If you live an average time then there are no winners or losers. At least that's the theory. But of course the amount of pension will be cut from that ideal by the profit the insurance company wants to make when people die according to average expectations. It will also be cut again to reflect the uncertainty about how long we are going to live, especially the recent evidence that there seems to be no end to the growth in the length of our lives. And it also reflects the investment returns that are available – because your declining pension fund stays invested and grows even after you have retired.

As life lengthens and investment returns fall, you won't be surprised to hear that the amount of annuity paid for a given fund has fallen by half over the last 20 years. Today a man aged 65 with £100,000 in his pension fund could get a fixed guaranteed income for life of around £6,500. Twenty years ago he could have got around £13,000. And experts say that lengthening life and growing uncertainty mean that the amounts will fall further in future.

You can buy an annuity as young as 50 if you want. But you would get very little. First, your fund is smaller because you have stopped paying into it. Second, it has to last longer. At 50 even pessimistic estimates give you 30 years of life rather than the comparable 20 years you have at 60 (again conservative estimates). So the longer you can put off crystallising your benefits (aka retiring), the bigger your pension because (a) you will be paying more in (b) what you have paid in will be growing for longer and (c) the pension you draw will have to last less time.

Assuming that the money in your pension fund grows by 5% a year after charges and you pay in a fixed amount each year, it will be twice as big after 30 years as it is after 20 years, and twice as big again after 42 years. So retiring at 72 will give you four times the pension fund you had at 50, even if your contributions stay the same.

And the fund you have will buy far more if you are 70 than if you are 60, or especially if you are 50. The amount varies depending on the type of annuity but roughly speaking, with an inflation-proofed annuity you will get a third more by waiting from 50 to 60, and a half more again by waiting until you are 70. Waiting from 50 to 70 will double your annuity when you finally get it. And as you will already have four times as much in your fund, waiting until 70 will give you eight times the pension you would get at 50.

You might think all this is leading up to saying that you should put off converting your pension fund into an annuity until as late as possible. And many advisers will tell you to do just that. The traditional advice is to wait as long as you can to boost the amount of your annuity. It's common sense. But it's wrong. As so often happens, arithmetic – helped by those A-Day changes – tells us something very different from the immediate reaction of our brain.

A couple of easy things should make us worry about the advice. First, eight times as much is a top-end result. It could be far less than that – three or four times might be more realistic. The other problem is that annuity rates have fallen and are likely to fall again. The rates I have used are the ones which were current when I wrote this book. Those are not the ones you will get. If you are 50 now then the rate you get now at 50 will be the 2006 rate. The rate you get at 60 will be the 2016 rate and the rate at 70 will be the 2026 rate. If you are 40 add ten years to each of these, and if you are 30 add 20 years. No-one knows what annuity rates will be in 2046 when today's 30 year olds are 70. But the expert view is that life expectancy is going to grow. And returns on investments are not going to get much better than they are now. So delaying almost inevitably means that annuity rates will be worse.

But the main problem is that you give a lot up if you defer claiming your annuity. You give up all the income you would have had for those years. Suppose you are 55 and you could claim your annuity now or put it off to 60 or 65. You do not want to stop work but we are talking benefit crystallisation here. You are also a man (we'll look at women later).

A man aged 55 with a £100,000 fund will get a top annuity of £5,793 a year. If he waits five years he will get £6,336, which is £543 a year more. That five years' wait has cost him 5 × £5,793 = £28,965. From when he does retire at 60 he will get an extra £543 a year, so it will take him 28,965/543 = 53.3 years before he will have had as much money as if he had not delayed by five years. He will be 113. The figures for delaying another five years are a bit better. He will get £7,103 which is £1,310 more a year. But over the ten years he has lost £57,930 and that will take him 57,930/1,310 = 44.2 years – when he is 109 – to get as much as if he had retired at 55.

But hang on a minute, what about the investment growth? Don't worry. You can get that too. Because remember retirement isn't about stopping work. It is about crystallising benefits. And if you are still working and earning at least as much as your annuity, you can put the whole income into another pension plan. So you can put that £5,793 straight into another pension (and don't get too excited about tax relief because the income will be taxed and you will get tax relief so the total amount going into your pension fund will be the same £5,793). Let's assume that grows by just 4% a year after charges. After ten years your new pension fund will be £78,126. You can then use that to buy an annuity which will be around £5,204 at today's rates. So at 65 you will get the original £5,793 + the new £5,204 which is £10,997 a year for the rest of your life, instead of the £7,103 you would have got if you had waited. So you are £3,894 a year better off – for life.

So claiming your annuity as soon as you can and reinvesting it at once in a pension is better than waiting. At least that is the arithmetic now. Of course that may change. The doomsday scenario is that your money does not grow at all, which means you would have £63,723, and that annuity rates plummet to around 30% of what they are now. Only then would you be worse off by taking this course of action. Of course it could happen. As could world peace.

CHOOSING AN ANNUITY

Whenever you decide to buy your annuity, you want to make sure you get the very best. I know choosing an annuity is not as exciting as picking out a new outfit or wondering which flat-screen TV is the best value or choosing the paint colours for your living room (magnolia's very safe if you are about to sell). But the right choice can make you richer for the rest of your life. Which is a smidge more important than whether you buy Sony or Panasonic. And if you make the right choice you'll be able to change that old early-21st century screen when you want.

You can buy an annuity off any insurance company that sells them. It does not have to be – and should not be – the company that nurtured your pension fund for you. It is like buying electricity. Your local sup-plier is always more expensive than the others. The worst annuity provider can give you around 20% less than the best. And once you have bought it, you cannot take it back or swap if you find a better deal. Buying an annuity is normally a once-for-a-lifetime choice. If you have £100,000 fund, choosing the right supplier can give you an extra £1,000 a year for life. It is called the Open Market Option, and for some reason is never abbreviated to OMO.

So rule two is use the open market option and find the best annuity. But before you do that, check out rule one. Some people, especially those with a pension plan that was begun before the early 1990s, may have a guarantee on the annuity they will be paid. When they were set these guarantees looked very low and were of course very cheap to offer. But they did allow the salesperson to mumble the word 'guarantee' and that, even out of context, leads to a warm and cheque-signing feeling in the mark – sorry customer. These sales techniques have come back to bite the firms that offered them. Because all the experts underestimated life expectancy and over-estimated investment returns, these guarantees are now well worth having and could give you a pension which is 40% higher than even the best you could buy on the market. So before you buy an annuity anywhere else, check if you have guarantees. And if you do, use them. And if you find out in time, consider sticking a lot more money into your pension before you crystallise those benefits.

> ### Rule of Prosperity
>
> **Always use the open market option when it comes to buying an annuity. But not if you have guaranteed annuity rates with your pension.**

So with rule one out of the way, proceed to rule two – but slowly. Because on the way you have to make various choices.

Do you want your annuity flat rate, or rising each year to help cope with inflation? A flat annuity will be fixed for life and so, after 20 years of inflation, will be worth far less than at the start. If inflation is around 3% a year, the value of money halves in 20 years. Instead of a flat annuity you can pick one that will go up each year to stave off the effects of price rise. The choice is either a fixed 3% or 5% extra each year, or you can choose one which will rise with prices. At the moment these index-linked annuities use the older measure of infla-tion – the Retail Prices Index, though that may be changed to the Consumer Prices Index in the future.

In some ways an inflation-proofed annuity is the ideal way to go. However long you live it will maintain its value in real terms. If it would buy you a new suit and a loaf of bread each week at the start, it would still do that in 40 years' time. It is often referred to as the risk-free option. But in fact it comes with a very heavy price. Because an annuity which rises each year will start a lot lower than a flat annuity.

And it will take a good few years before it reaches the level of the flat one. For example, a man aged 65 with £100,000 can buy a flat annuity of £7,103 year today. If he chooses to have a 3% rise each year, it will start nearly £2,000 a year less at £5,180. Growing at 3% a year it will be year 12 (when he is 77) before the annual payment catches up with the flat rate of £7,103. And it will be year 22 (when he is 87) before the total amount he has been paid becomes equal. Most people aged 65 will not live to cross that break even point. If he picks a 5% rise each year and starts with £4,090, the crossover points are year 13 before he gets more than £7,103 a year, and it is again year 22 before he has received more money altogether.

If he wants to take risk out of it altogether and have his pension rise with inflation, as the state pension and many company pensions do, then the arithmetic tells an even worse story. If inflation stays around 2.5% then he will have to wait until year 17 – if he lives that long – to get back to the level of his original pension. And year 31 (when he will be 96) before he has received more altogether. That's because no-one knows what the level of inflation is going to be, so the insurance company adds a bit on for its risk that it might turn out to be 10% or 15% in future. In fact the arithmetic shows they reckon it will average around 3.5% a year, not 2.5%.

Given that money now is worth more than money in the future, the real value of these lower pensions is even less. So although in the past cautious old me has said to people that they should always choose an inflation-proofed pension, when I did the arithmetic I realised that there is a very big risk with that advice that you will end up worse off. Choosing a flat annuity does carry its own risk – that you will live a long time and end up worse off in your very old age, should you reach it. But having done the sums, I will not be going for a rising annuity.

Impaired life is the attractive phrase used by insurers for people who smoke or have a disease which is expected to shorten their life. They will then get a higher annuity than someone who has no reason to expect that their life will be shortened. Sometimes they are split into two categories – enhanced rates for minor things such as smoking, asthma, high blood pressure and so on. And impaired life rates for major diseases like cancer, Parkinson's, HIV/AIDS, or kidney disease. They can easily be double the rate paid to people without such conditions. Enhanced rates for smokers (at least ten a day for ten years) come at the bottom of the enhancements and are only about 1% to 3% higher than standard rates. But if you feel you may be in one of these categories, it is important to get specialist financial advice to make sure you get the best rate going. One estimate suggests that four out of ten retired people could get an enhanced rate, but only about one in ten actually applies for one.

One life or two – If you are married or live with a partner, you can ensure that the annuity continues to be paid to them if you die first. Before you make this choice, consult them first. It is only really necessary if that person is financially dependent on you. This choice will reduce the income from your annuity. The reduction will depend on the age and sex of your partner, and how much you want them to inherit – half, two thirds, or all of it. As an example, a man of 60 with a £100,000 fund who has a 55-year-old wife and wants her to have two thirds of the annuity if he dies first would get £5,626 instead of £6,336, a reduction of about 11%.

Guaranteed or not – Annuities are a once-for-lifetime deal. If you die within a year or two of taking it out, your whole fund has disappeared for a year or two's pension. The insurance company has done very well on its bet. But the heirs of the person making it might feel rather annoyed. So the insurers have come up with a good wheeze: another bet – this time that you will not die within, say, five years. The stake is a smaller annuity for life. And the prize is that your payments will continue for at least five years. If you do die in that time, then your heirs get the payments. Strangely – or perhaps not – the guarantee is not very expensive. So much so that the best rates for an annuity with a guaranteed period can be better than those without a guaranteed period.

Market related – The whole essence of an annuity is that it is guaranteed – a pension for life that you can rely on. OK it may not be that much and there are choices and difficulties on the way, but once you've got one it is there – forever. Or at least as long a you are. But a few years ago, as rates for annuities fell, insurance companies came up with a bright idea. Always beware bright ideas from insurance companies. Instead of locking you into an actuary's cautious view of investment returns over the next 30 years, the insurer offered you an annuity that was 'market related'. If the value of shares on the stock market grew, then so would your annuity! Hurray. And if they fell, your annuity would fall too. Though they didn't always tell you that bit quite as loudly. These annuities were always a bad idea and should always be avoided. And before you write to me with an account of Uncle Charles who got twice as much as he would have had with a standard annuity, first check with UC and get some paperwork to back up his story, and second remember that someone wins the National Lottery each week despite the odds of 14 million to one. And Camelot prefers talking about the winners than the losers too.

ANNUITIES ARE HISTORY – NEW A-DAY CHOICES

Now I've explained all about annuities you can forget them – for a while. Because since A-Day, annuities are history. If you want them to be. Personally I don't think you should. Annuities are a true reflection of the market value of money over the remainder of the human life-time. Yes they involve profit and yes there is a ton of caution built in, but they do genuinely move up and down to reflect changes in life expectancy (lengthening) and investment returns (which are getting better at the moment).

But the A-Day revolution does give you a choice. Not a simple choice, but a choice.

As long as you are under 75, you need not buy an annuity. Instead you can choose to take what is called 'unsecured income'. The money in the fund has to remain invested and of course money labelled 'annual management charge' will still drip out of the hole in the bottom of your pension pot. But you can withdraw money from it to live on, up to a maximum amount. The calculation of that amount is very complicated and is not related to real annuities but to tables produced by the Government Actuary. But it is around the amount you could get from a flat rate single life annuity, plus a fifth. So if your pension fund could buy you an annuity of £1,000 a year, you can take 120% of that, which is £1,200 a year, out of it. But using this approximation a 65-year-old woman (I said we'd come on to the women later) could get £6,662 for her £100,000 fund, so she can take an 'unsecured income' from it of £6,662 × 1.2 = £7,994. That is the maximum. And of course like an annuity payment, it is taxed. But there is no minimum. So if you want, you can just leave your pension fund to grow (minus charges) and draw zero from it. The old pre-A-Day rule that you had to draw a minimum income has gone. And if you (or your Uncle Charles) had what was called a drawdown scheme, that will have become an unsecured income scheme on 6 April 2006.

The advantage of the unsecured income over the annuity is that the fund itself remains yours. You have not given it to the insurance company, so it can be inherited if you die – though minus 35% tax – and if you want to change what it is invested in then you can go ahead.

Alternatively, you can use some of your pension fund to buy a new product called a short-term annuity. Now I know an annuity is defined as 'an income for life', but a short-term annuity is not for life; it is, well, for a short term, a fixed period of up to five years. And the period cannot go beyond your 75th birthday. The rest of the fund can be used by you later or, if you die, inherited subject to the 35% tax.

Once you reach 75 this unsecured income has to come to an end. At that time your choices are very limited. You can, of course, convert your fund into an annuity and that will probably be the best choice – see earlier remarks about the market accuracy of annuities. Or, if you still want to be in charge of it, you can take what is called an 'alternative secured pension' – an ASP. All that means is that you can withdraw money from your fund as before, but with one big difference. Instead of letting you take out 120% of the amount you could get if you bought an annuity, once you reach 75 you will only be able to draw 70%. And it is 70% of the annuity you can buy with what is left of your fund. If you have been drawing the maximum unsecured income, that may be relatively little.

The advantage over buying an annuity is that, once more, the diminishing capital remains yours – but not to do what you like with. When you die you cannot just leave the remains of the fund to your heirs. You have to transfer it to the pension fund of a spouse, a child under 21 or a dependant, such as disabled family member you support. Alternatively, it can be transferred to the pension fund of another member in the same scheme. If none of that is possible, you can choose to leave it tax free to charity.

Why, you may ask, should you pass it on to another member of your scheme? You always fancied that chap in accounts, but leave him your pension? I don't think so. In fact this is a mechanism for wealthy families to pass money tax free between generations. They can set up a 'family pension fund' which all family members can join and then leave the remains of their fund to that fund. This rule is unlikely to be much use for ordinary folk of ordinary means. What else do you expect from changes by a Labour Government?

BOOSTING YOUR CASH LUMP SUM

The annuity, unsecured income and the alternative secured income are just part of the benefits you get on retirement. You have to use three quarters of your pension fund to buy them. But a quarter can be taken as cash. Yes cash. So if your pension fund is £100,000 you can take £25,000 as cash. Yes cash. Tax-free cash. Have I said cash enough yet? Because it's more money, in cash, than most of us will ever see. Of course, when I say cash I don't mean you have to take it in used tenners (though that might be nice, mightn't it?). Just a nice big cheque.

First the rules. Unlike the pre-A-Day position, the rules are simple. Whatever your pension fund you can take 25% of it, no more no less, as cash. However, if you had an entitlement to more than that, which a few might have done, before A-Day then you should be able to draw that amount. It is up to your pension scheme administrator or provider to have kept a note of what you were entitled to. Or you could have registered it as part of applying for enhanced or primary protection (see p. 141 above)

If you are a member of a salary-related scheme the rules are, guess what, incredibly complicated. I had heard, and indeed used, the phrase 'eye-wateringly difficult'. But one pension expert I consulted told me that they were even worse – 'nose-bleedingly difficult', he said. Which made it very difficult to read the briefing he sent me. But as far as I can see, the overall result is that it is probably not a good idea to take the maximum cash. You could find your pension cut by a third or more, rather than by the quarter you might expect. Best thing is to ask for a range of tax-free cash options and the effect on your pension, and choose the balance that suits you best. But do remember that the pension you give up is going to be raised each year in line with inflation, or at least parts of it are, up to certain limits. And someone else is paying for that.

Right. So. You have got your tax-free lump sum. And although it is cash, and there is no tax to pay on it, you shouldn't just keep it at home and spend it. No the cash is there for a purpose – to earn you still more money. Or of course to pay off debt (see Chapter 8). Paying off debt in your 50s is a really good use for this cash. And debt includes your mortgage – because in case you hadn't noticed, it is the biggest debt most of us ever have and although etc etc, it is still a debt and a lump of cash can cut that debt and help secure your financial security in retirement. And this time by 'retirement' I do mean when you give up work and live on the money you've saved up over your working life.

There are all sorts of things you can do with this money and almost as many IFAs trying to get it off you. Not to keep all of it you understand, just some of it.

So I am going to concentrate on the pensiony-type things you can do with it – in fact just one of them. An annuity. No no no, it's not boring and it's not the same as the annuities we discussed earlier. I know it's the same name and it is the same principle – you give an insurance company a lump sum (your tax-free cash) and it promises you an income for life – but it is better. Because part of the income is tax free.

When you buy a pension you have bought it using tax-free income. So the pension you turn it into is taxed as income. But if you buy an annuity with another sort of money, perhaps you have saved it up or inherited it, then most of the money you get each month is just the return of that capital. And even the Revenue is not going to tax you on that. You are just taxed on the bit that the boffins at the Revenue reckon your lump sum has earned. So if you did want to convert your whole pension fund into an annuity, it is better to buy a pension annuity with three quarters of it and what is called a 'purchased life annuity' (and it's too old a phrase to merit its own TLA so don't call it a PLA) with your quarter tax-free cash.

Here's how it works. Say you are 60 and you have £100,000 in your fund (and if you don't, it's easy to scale it up – or down). You don't smoke and you want payments guaranteed for five years even if you die before that. If you spent the whole £100,000 on a pension annuity you would get £6,256 (these figures are a bit different from others in the book. That is because annuity rates change from day to day and these were done at a different time). That will be taxed, so let's say you pay tax at the basic rate on all of it. You end up with just £4,880 a year. But if you take the tax-free cash, you have £75,000 to buy a pension annuity, you get £4,689 a year and after tax at 22%, that works out at £3,657 a year to spend. The other £25,000 you use to buy a purchased life annuity and you get from that £1,393 a year after tax has been deducted. Add them up and you get £5,050 – so you're £170 a year better off for just a little bit of thought.

CHAPTER TEN

Help! I'm Lost – Going out on a limb without losing an arm and a leg

FINANCIAL ADVICE

There are 489 different sorts of financial adviser. Really. And that is without dividing them into competent/incompetent or honest/dishonest or whether they are paid by a fee or by commission. Or both. There used to be two kinds. Independent financial advisers and tied agents. Independents advised about the whole market. Tied agents could only sell the products of one company. It was easy to explain. In fact most journalists and commentators just said

independent = good

tied = bad

and that was it. Because tied agents could only advise you about the products of one company, the one they worked for, whereas IFAs were obliged to search the whole market for all the products available and find you the best one for your needs. So tied bad, independent good. Who could disagree with that?

Well, the Financial Services Authority. It decided that the system needed to be modernised, freed up and made more competitive, or what they said was 'less anti-competitive' which might be the same thing. Unnecessary restrictions had to be removed. And before you knew it there were nine sorts of financial adviser for investments. And they could choose to be paid in three ways – fee, commission or both (but we will ignore that because it makes 27 different sorts and you finally get to a calculation which shows that there are 4731 different kinds of financial adviser. That's so silly you probably wouldn't believe me, so we'll stick with what mathematicians call an approximation.) Then mortgage brokers were added and there are six sorts of them. And six months later insurance agents came under the FSA, adding another six kinds of adviser who sell insurance. And any adviser can be in any of the categories for each product. So there are 9 x 6 x 6 = 324 kinds of adviser who sells all three products and 144 who sell two sorts and 21 who sell just one sort which makes a grand total of 489 different kinds (and remembering that if we hadn't done that approximation we would have found 4731 different kinds). And because you couldn't really call them all by different names, they can all call themselves 'financial adviser'. In fact they can call themselves anything which is not misleading. So they could describe themselves as 'the money bloke' or 'that nice woman who sells financial stuff' though they could not call themselves 'the guaranteed 12% return company' or 'cheapest mortgages finder'. Only one category in each group can add the word 'independent' to that phrase and become the acronymic IFA. Which does not stand for I Flog Anything but Independent Financial Adviser.

They are still the only ones you should go to for advice. Let me explain who the others are.

First, to the original two sorts

* tied – selling products just of one company, and
* independent – selling products from all companies

a third type was inserted in the middle. In the business this group is known as 'multi-tied' and that means they can only sell the products of a limited group of companies with whom they have done a deal. These companies are called their panel and it can be any size from two to 20 or more. But however big it is they are restricted to the products of just those companies, and if a product that is cheaper or better suited to your needs is sold by a company that is not on their panel, they are not allowed to tell you about it – still less sell it to you. So their advice is limited. It is like going to a Renault dealer and asking for a Nissan. It ain't gonna happen. And even worse, while a Renault dealer will happily compare his product – favourably of course – with a Nissan, tied and multi-tied are not allowed to make any comparison at all or discuss the products they are not tied to.

So three types. That doesn't sound too bad. But these three – tied, multi and independent – are then split in three the other way.

At the top are the full-blown genuine advisers. They are trained and have to be qualified, or at least of long-standing experience, to be approved by the FSA. They can give you advice, but of course if they are tied or multi-tied that advice is limited to the companies they are tied to. These advisers are all individually authorised by the Financial Services Authority. Which means you can look them up on its website to check (a) if they are authorised and (b) if any disciplinary action has been taken against them. If they are not authorised avoid them like the plague. They are breaking the law. If action has been taken against them treat them like a severe case of the flu. Only enter the room if you really have to.

Under them is a new breed of adviser who is not qualified and not individually authorised to do their job. So you cannot check up on them on the FSA website. But the company they work for must be authorised, so you can check up on that at least. Because this lot are by definition incompetent, they are only allowed to sell you products which are branded 'stakeholder'. If you are offered such an adviser you should politely ask for someone who is qualified, or politely leave and go to a different adviser. You might as well pick your own stake-holder product and save money.

You do that by going to the third band of advisers. They don't give advice at all. Yes, they are called financial advisers, some even independent financial advisers, but they don't give advice. It's like expecting a sleeping policeman to arrest someone. Or a cricket bat to fly around in the dark catching insects. The term 'adviser' is just what they are called, not what they are. Technically they are called 'execution only' advisers. Because you do your research, decide what you want and then they just sell it to you. So who do they execute? Pass.

Here are the nine types of financial adviser for pensions and investments in a table.

	Independent	Multi-tied	Tied
Qualified and authorised	Advise on and sell you all investment products	Advise and sell you all products from a small range of providers with whom they have done deals on commission rates	Advise and sell you all products from one provider only
Unqualified and unauthorised	Sell you stakeholder pensions and investments from providers which the research department says are best	Sell you stakeholder pensions and investments from a small range of providers who have done deals on commission	Sell you a stakeholder product from one company
Execution only, company authorised	Offer no advice but fulfil your instructions to buy a product you have decided on	Offer no advice but fulfil your instructions to buy a product from a small range of providers who have done a deal on commission	Offer no advice and sell you one product

Now this is a theoretical table – all nine cells filled, because we humans like things neat. Not all these categories may exist. But they could under the rules.

So how on earth do you tell what the person in front of you is? Here is what they will be called.

	Independent	Multi-tied	Tied
Qualified and authorised	Independent financial adviser	Financial adviser	Financial adviser
Execution only, company authorised	Independent financial adviser	Financial adviser	Financial adviser
Unqualified and unauthorised	Financial adviser	Financial adviser	Financial adviser

So that doesn't help much. But now by law they have to give you a bit of paper that will. This bit of paper will be headed '**key**facts about our services'. Note the use of the new word 'keyfacts' which is 'key facts' without the space, making it into one word rather than two. And then separating the two words by using bold for the first three letters. This has to be printed to look like this, with a jaunty pokey bit at the bottom.

Then there will be a heading 'Whose products do we offer?' Here is what it says and what it means.

What **key**facts says	What it means
We offer products from the whole market.	Independent financial adviser.
We only offer products from a limited number of companies. Ask us for a list of companies and products we offer.	Multi-tied financial adviser. Remember they are tied to selling the products of a small group of companies they have chosen, partly on grounds of how much commission they are paid.
We only offer products from a single group of companies (or it might give the name of the company or just say 'we only offer our own products').	Tied financial adviser. They can only sell products from one company or group.

By one of the three boxes will be a tick. Make sure it is by the top box. So that deals with the three columns in my table on p. 181. What about the rows? **key**facts will set these out next under 'which service will we provide you with'.

What **key**facts says	What it means
We will advise and make a recommendation for you after we have assessed your needs.	These are qualified and individually registered financial advisers from the top row of my table above. They can sell investment or pension products from any company.
You will not receive advice or a recommendation from us. We may ask some questions to narrow down the selection of products	These are execution only advisers. They are qualified and registered. But they just carry out your instructions.

that we will provide details on. You will then need to make your own choice about how to proceed.	
We will provide basic advice on a limited range of stakeholder products and in order to do this we will ask some questions about your income, savings and other circumstances but we will not: ★ **conduct a full assessment of your needs;** ★ **offer advice on whether a non-stakeholder product may be more suitable.**	The person sitting opposite you is not qualified to sell financial products. They are not registered individually with the FSA. They are only allowed to sell stakeholder products with low costs and limited risks which may or may not be suitable for you.

So these are the three rows in my table above. Again, make sure the top box is ticked.

So when you get given **key**facts, check that the two boxes ticked are the top rows in each case. Then you will have an independent financial adviser who can act on your behalf and sell you any product that is suitable from any provider. The only exception is if you are really confident that you can pick the product you want and are happy to buy it from an execution only agent. Remember you have no redress if things go wrong, no compensation scheme and no way of claiming mis-selling. In that case go for Top Box and Middle Box. And cross your fingers.

And there is another trap awaiting the unwary in this new simplified system. (You could at this point go back to p. 3, cut out the word 'complexified' and stick it over the word 'simplified' in the previous sentence.) My table contains a scandalous approximation. I implied that advisers who tick the top box in both sets of information – 'whole of market' and 'we will advise you' – were all independent financial advisers. And in a sense they are. But they have to pass one more test to be able to call themselves that. More on that later.

Sometimes the **key**facts document will also list similar choices separately for insurance advice and mortgage advice, if your adviser also sells those products. But there are only two rows. There are no stakeholder mortgage or insurance products (yet), so the unqualified and unregistered row does not happen. Which is good. But the bad thing is that any adviser can be independent for investment but tied or multitied for insurance or mortgages. Ties for insurance are particularly common, regardless of the status of the adviser for investment products or mortgages.

And there is another nasty trick awaiting you on the insurance front. Often advisers will not only be tied but they will tick the box that means they do not give you advice either. In other words they are happy to consider the whole market and give you advice about a pension. But when it comes to insurance, they will take the commission but only flog one company's products and not even advise you about it. It is what is called a 'non-advised sale' and at some stage you will sign a document saying you know and accept that the insurance bit is unadvised. Even though the person sitting opposite you calls themselves an adviser. Whether you realise you have signed it or the implications of doing so are less certain.

A third nasty trick when it comes to buying insurance will be saved for later revelation.

CHOOSING AN IFA
Once you have got rid of any thought of plain old financial advisers and unqualified advisers you will still be left with about 27,000 individuals who are registered and, to varying extents, qualified, and who hold themselves out to be independent financial advisers.

How on earth do you choose one among so many? That is a difficult problem. But it is made a bit easier nowadays by an organisation called Independent Financial Adviser Promotion. Its website is called www.unbiased.co.uk and I have to be honest that both names put me off. But it is an organisation that has one very good service. You can use its database to find a local IFA who specialises in one of 17 kinds of product. And each IFA is only allowed to have three specialities, to cut out the smart alecs who claim to specialise in everything. Remember that 'personal protection' means insurance not bodyguards. Just tick the two relating to pensions and proceed.

You can also limit your search to IFAs who have an extra qualification in that speciality – though you can only pick one and the website doesn't help you to understand which qualification is best; that would take another week or so research (or you can just read the paragraph below). You can also choose a female – or a male – adviser if that would make you feel more comfortable, and restrict your search if you want to those with an email or website. Never trust anyone in business without a website is my motto. Mine is www.paullewis.co.uk by the way.

Like everything else in financial services, the qualifications that people have to do their job are hard to understand. Every IFA has to have at least one qualification – it comes in various forms, but the most common one was called the Financial Planning Certificate and has now been modernised and renamed the Certificate in Financial Planning. Needless to say these can be abbreviated to a TLA, i.e. FPC and CFP. There is also the Certificate for Financial Advisers or CeFA. If anyone tries to bamboozle you with these as qualifications, ignore them. It's like a doctor saying they have a medical degree. Of course they have.

What you want is extra stuff. There are eight bodies that set exams and give qualifications (though some of them are subsidiaries of each other) and there are more than 30 different qualifications an IFA might have (apart from the FPC or CFP and useful things like GCSE maths or English which not all of them appear to have begun). Here we are only concerned with the six pension qualifications, though you should also note that the biggest group of qualifications are the so-called 'generic' ones that act as some sort of overall quality control. It is better to pick someone who is an 'associate' or, better still, a 'fellow' of the Personal Finance Society (part of the Chartered Insurance Institute), the Institute of Financial Planning or the Pensions Management Institute. That means they have passed lots of 'modules' in the exams so they know a lot of stuff, including usually some extra pension qualifications. As for the specifics, four are from the Chartered Insurance Institute. The G60 is the main add-on pensions qualification which covers nearly all the pensions topics; CF9 is specifically about the changes that started on A-Day. You should make sure your adviser has both of these. K10 and K20 are extras on top of those – one about retirement options and one about investment in retirement. The APMI – Associate of the Pensions Management Institute – is more for people in the professional management of pensions or staff than it is for IFAs. IFA Promotions has a useful guide if you want to pursue this esoteric subject called *Your Guide to IFA Qualifications* QUAL03, or you could contact the Financial Services Skills Council.

MEETING UP

So you've found a local IFA who specialises in pensions and has extra qualifications and, better still, doesn't live too far away from you. You call to make an appointment. Some will offer to visit you. Never let an Independent Financial Adviser into your home. The same rule as applies to bailiffs and vampires. Once you invite them across the threshold they can take your furniture and suck your blood. And bailiffs and vampires aren't that nice either.

Whoops! No seriously folks, never let any salesman into your home. It is much better to visit their office. First you get a clear impression of how they work – what their place is like. If they have very expensive offices in the smart part of town and several good-looking young things who do very little except say hello and make coffee, ask yourself who is paying for all that unnecessary expense. If they have one helper in an untidy place up bare stairs over a kebab shop, ask yourself if they are really any good. It's a hard balance but you must find someone you trust and like. If you don't like the look of them you can leave as soon as it is not too impolite to do so.

But if they come to your home it is very hard to get rid of them when you want. And if you have given them tea and biscuits and seen the pictures of their kids (or someone's) in their wallet, it is very hard to say 'no'. Or even 'I'll think about it'.

If you do ignore this rule (deep sigh), always remember that you will be able to cancel any pension contract you sign if you do it within a cooling-off period. Nowadays that is 30 days. The pension provider will write to you telling you that and if you write back within 30 days of the date on that letter, the deal is undone. And my advice – sorry, there is always more advice – is never sign anything on your first meeting anyway. Get lots of material, take it away and think about it.

Because every financial adviser worth his or her salt (what does that phrase mean?) will give you a first session free anyway, so you can suss each other out. Remember, the deal you are about to do here will cost you more than your last outfit, more than your hi-fi, more than your sofa, more than your car, possibly eventually almost as much as your house. So give it a bit of care please.

Because the first meeting is free, see two or three advisers. And pick the one that you chime with best. Here are a few danger signals.

* **Do they ask you about any debts you have? If not, do not trust their advice.**
* **If you have a debt (other than a mortgage), do they discuss paying it off before you buy a pension? If not, politely leave.**
* **Do they offer you exceptional returns on an investment? I hate to repeat myself, but if it seems too good to be true, it probably is. Leave now.**
* **Can they explain the details of what they are offering clearly and WSA (without stupid acronyms)? If you ask for a further explanation, do they just repeat what they have just said? If no to the first and yes to the second question, walk away.**
* **Do you feel they know what they are talking about? If not, ask a few questions and if you still feel the same, leave.**
* **Do they say that the offer is running out and if you don't say yes at once you might miss it? Always a sign of a con. Run out.**
* **Do they suggest cashing in your existing pension and moving it to a new one? This could be what is called 'churning' – moving your investments so they can earn interest for a new sale. It's against the law but, hey, so is speeding and a lot of that goes on.**

★ **Are they paying attention to diversity and asset allocation?**
In other words, are all your eggs going in one basket labelled
'shares', or, as they always prefer to call them 'equities'. If
they are not spreading your risk, question them closely.

★ **Do they ask you to make the cheque for your investment out
to them or their firm? Never do that.** Always make it out to
the financial institution you are investing with. The only
exception is for a fee. In that case wait for the bill – and
make sure you are happy with the advice – before you pay
it.

> **Rule of Prosperity**
>
> **Choose your financial adviser carefully, try out several, and never
> let them into your home.**

keyfacts

They will all of course give you a **key**facts document. And remember
to make sure they tick the top box in each case for (a) independent
(products from the whole market) and (b) financial adviser (we will
advise and recommend). There is another choice to be made too: how
they are paid. By a fee or by commission. In other words, do you get
out your cheque book or debit card and pay a bill for their time, or do
you let them be paid by the company that manufactures the products
they are selling to you?

There is a separate **key**facts document which sets out how the
adviser is paid called '**key**facts about the cost of our services'. The
paragraph 'What are your payment options' has two boxes to show if
the adviser is paid by a fee or by commission. Advisers can tick either
or both of these boxes. To be independent the adviser must tick the
'paying by fee' box. They can also tick the 'paying by commission'
box, which means you have a choice. But if they only tick that box
then they cannot call themselves 'independent' even if they ticked
the earlier boxes to show they can sell products from the 'whole of
market'.

In the past many IFAs would joke that they didn't care if people wanted to pay a fee or by commission, as long as they were paid. Ha ha. And today, although the rules say that all IFAs have to allow payment by fee, most also say they may be paid by commission. And the two methods get very blurred.

Commission is so deep seated in the financial services industry that it is difficult for the IFA not to be paid commission. So if they are paid commission anyway, what is the point of paying a fee? And this is where the blurredness comes in. They will say that the two methods are really much the same. They work out a fee for their time. The pension provider then pays them commission. And they 'offset' one against the other. So if their fee is £1,000 and the commission is £1,100 then you pay no fee and the extra £100 is used to put a bit more into your pension.

It seems like the best of both worlds. But don't be fooled.

First a word about commission. Everyone knows that sales people get commission. When you go into a shop and buy a dress or a DVD player, the sales assistant gets something from the money you pay. It might be a fiver or £20 but you don't mind because the service was good and it is part of the price and it is so much nicer to shop in a shop rather than save a bit of money by buying online. So what is wrong with commission in financial services? Like the services themselves, it is much more complicated and much more expensive.

There are several types of commission. First there is the obvious 'initial commission' – the fee the adviser gets for selling you the product in the first place. Second there is 'renewal commission'. If you commit yourself to paying a monthly premium then the adviser may get a small percentage of that too as long as you keep paying in. Third there is what is called 'trail commission', which is a small percentage of the total value of your pension fund. So if you are in the fund for 40 years your adviser will be getting commission not just when he or she sells the deal to you, but every month and year thereafter until you retire. So far so relatively simple. But initial commission can be paid as renewal commission. Suppose you commit yourself to paying £100 a month into a pension. The salesperson will get £245 initial commission, but spread over 12 months. So out of each of your £100 payments, £20 will go to the salesperson. In addition they will get 1/400th – a quarter of one percent – of the value of your fund for ever. This payment will start at £3 (1/4% of £1,200) but as your fund grows to become £100,000 they will get £250 a year out of it. Now in fact this money does not come direct from your invest-ment. It comes out of the charges that are made by the provider to you – the initial 5% they may charge you (though many don't) and the 1.5% a year they take out of your pension fund.

So far so sort of simple. But there are other forms of commission. For example, the trail commission can be paid up front. So instead of getting a few pounds a year for 40 years, the IFA will get that money up front – a lot less of course than if it was paid over 40 years, but if any industry can work out what is called the 'net present value' of money due to be paid in the future it is the insurance industry. And if the customer does not stay with the product for a minimum period, say five or even ten years, then it can be taken back by the insurance company. And that is just one of the complexities of commission. One industry estimate says there are 1,200 different 'shapes' of commission.

For example, in 2004 a Norwich Union stakeholder pension where you paid in one lump sum of say £10,000 would pay commission of (a) 2.5% of the premium which is £250, or (b) 0.4% of the fund value each year for as long as you keep it: that works out as £40 in year one and more each subsequent year as the fund grows – assuming it does (note that this is worth more than £250 if you keep the plan for around five years). Or (c) a combination of the two which pays 1% upfront and 0.3% a year, which is £100 + £30 in year one and that £30 will grow as the fund grows for as long as you keep it.

These fees come out of the 1% a year you paid to Norwich Union. If your IFA asks for the non-commission sale then the 1% charge is reduced to 0.6%.

So it is not really like the tenner earned for selling a DVD player. Understanding commission and its effects is a study in itself. But it can amount to a very large amount of money indeed.

And because it is so complicated it can be hard to be sure that the IFA is going to return to you all the different bits of commission in exchange for the fee. The upfront commission will always be returned (though I did hear of one IFA who charged his clients a fee, a big one, *and* kept the commission. He said that the fee was for his brain work, the commission was for the sale). But the renewal commission and especially the trail commission may not be.

But that is not the main reason why you should not offset the fee against commission. My spectacles sharpen the blurred image like this. You get the advice now. So you should pay now for it. Remember the Rule of Prosperity on debt (Chapter 8)? Never borrow the money to pay for something if the debt will last longer than what you have bought. You have bought advice from the IFA, not a pension. You buy that from the insurance company. So if the adviser charges you £1,000, pay it now. If you cannot afford that then borrow it and pay for it over, say, a year. And make sure that every penny you put into your pension is left there and not used to pay commission. Not just now but every year in the future.

And that can amount to a huge amount off the money you have invested.

Take that example of a pension that you pay £100 a month into. If you pay in for 25 years and it grows at 7% a year with charges of 1.5% a year, including commission, that would build up to a fund of £174,000 at the end of that period. If you buy it without commission, ie you pay your adviser a fee, those charges could be reduced to 0.6% a year. That means the fund will be £222,000. Which is £48,000 more for you Which could mean another £3000 a year for life on the annuity you buy.

The reason is that you are effectively borrowing the money for the fee by paying it out of your pension fund from now to retirement. And every pound paid out is a pound less earning interest, in that example for 25 years but in some cases for up to 40 years. So do not borrow your adviser's fee. At least not from them. If you cannot afford it now then borrow it from the bank over say two years. That will end up a lot cheaper.

Some advisers will tell you that if you pay the fee then VAT is due, but if you pay for it through commission there is no VAT. That is simply not true. And if someone does tell you that, you might wonder about the accuracy or honesty of everything else they tell you. If you are charged a fee for advice which is related to buying a product then no VAT is due. You do not have to buy anything to avoid the VAT. The advice just has to be capable of generating a sale. If the advice is, for example, about tax or could not involve buying anything, then VAT is due on it.

And one final thing on commission. The **key**facts document will show the commission that is charged by your adviser on a regular or a lump-sum investment into a pension. And it will compare that with the market average. Your adviser may charge more or less than that average. What it does not show is the actual commission on the product you actually buy – and that will affect the likelihood of it being sold. So the higher the commission the adviser earns, the more they will push that product.

Now before all the IFAs reading this splutter into their coffee and spit nails across the room, let me tell you why that is true. First, research for the Association of British Insurers about commission published in February 2005 found that sales of some products were biased by the commission paid in the case of about one in seven advisers. Second, insurance companies pay more commission on products they want to sell. Norwich Union, for example, slashed the commission on stake-holder pensions in 2005 because it wanted to sell fewer of them. And when a new product is brought to market, the commission is usually higher for a period of time. If commission did not affect sales, why would that be done? And that same research commissioned by the insurance industry found that by raising commission just half a percentage point, a company could increase its market share by 14 percentage points.

But the industry still likes to claim commission does not bias sales. Here is a short exchange in 2005 between me and David Severn, at the time the boss of the Association of Independent Financial Advisers. It is verbatim. So if bits don't seem to make sense you'll have to work out what he meant yourself.

LEWIS: 'Do you accept that higher commission does drive higher sales of those products?'

SEVERN: 'I think commission or bonuses attached to salary, all things, have some incentive effect on advisers whether they're independent or whether they're working for a bank.'

LEWIS: 'But you're drawing a distinction between incentive and bias?'

SEVERN: 'I think I am.'

Mmm. I failed to understand that then and I still cannot get my head round it now. How can it give an incentive and affect sales, without biasing them? Incidentally you can hear the programme that was taken from at www.bbc.co.uk/moneybox if you put 'sins of commission' in the search box.

So it is always better to cut the advice process free from the sales process, and pay a fee upfront for products that are commission free. Then you can be sure there is no bias and every penny you put in is for your benefit not the salesperson's. Of course, there will still be charges taken out of your fund. But it won't be commission and it won't bias the sale.

And what will the fee cost you? How long is a piece of string? Or more accurately, how long is a string of diamonds? IFAs will charge you £100 to £200 an hour. In London and big cities probably even more. It sounds a lot – OK it is a lot, a single mum with two kids will get £153 income support and tax credit to keep the three of them for a week – but it is much in line with what a solicitor or an accountant will charge. And you will have no way of knowing how your IFA's charge compares with the average because that is not shown on the **keyfacts** document. To do the work required to calculate what you need by way of a pension and sell it to you might take five hours or more, so reckon on up to £1,000. And before you say 'hang on a minute', what did you pay last time you moved house for surveys, lawyers, estate agents and removal? A lot more than that. And your pension is just as important.

MIS-SELLING

No-one, not even the most diehard supporter of the financial services industry, can pretend that pensions have not been widely mis-sold in the past. Nearly two million people were encouraged to leave good salary-related pension schemes for the costs of a personal pension invested among the vagaries of the stock market.

The total compensation was £11.5 billion and the cost of doing the full survey and administering the refunds was a further £2 billion.

Is it still going on? Well, probably not. Or not on this scale – and this book will help you avoid mis-sales. And if it turns out that you have been mis-sold something then there is a formal process to make a complaint and, if it is upheld, get compensation.

I will spare you the details – let's hope you never need them – but here is a brief outline of what to do if you think you were sold a pension wrongly or you were misled into buying a particular product.

★ Set out your complaint in writing to the boss of the firm you blame – normally the IFA. Explain what you think they should do about it.
★ If that does not produce the result you want then you can go to

the Financial Ombudsman Service (often called FOS). You can also do that if your case has reached what is called 'deadlock', which means you have not had a final reply within eight weeks of making the complaint.

★ The initial response from the Ombudsman will in fact be from an Assessor. Their job is to resolve disputes and it may be that you feel the response is not what you want. You can ask for your case to go to an Ombudsman for a formal decision. That can include redress for any loss and compensation.

★ The company has to follow the Ombudsman's decision and it cannot appeal against it directly. Some companies have attempted to challenge decisions in court on the grounds that the Ombudsman has behaved unreasonably, but no appeal on these grounds has, so far, been successful.

★ If you do not like the Ombudsman's decision you cannot appeal against it. But you can either:
  ★ take your case against the company directly to court – which will be expensive and you must be sure you have good legal grounds, or
  ★ complain about the Ombudsman's decision to the Independent Assessor. They cannot reverse the decision but can only consider the way the complaint was handled.

The Financial Ombudsman Service is extremely busy. In 2004/05 the number of complaints quadrupled to 110,000 (which may tell us something about the way the financial services industry behaves!) – though the number of complaints about pensions fell to 4,214 from 5,303 the year before. As complaints have grown, staff numbers have risen by rather less. So expect to wait six months for your complaint to be resolved.

Just to confuse things, there is also a Pensions Ombudsman. His job is to consider complaints about the way a pension scheme is run, not how a pension is sold. He is completely separate from the FOS and can take complaints about an employer's pension scheme or a personal pension if you think there has been maladministration or injustice which has caused you loss. He can order compensation. The two ombudsmen will sort out which of them should take your complaint if you go to the wrong one.

Neither Ombudsman can look at complaints about how an investment such as a pension has performed, unless you were misled about what to expect (FOS) or the poor performance was caused by maladministration (PO).

If a company goes out of business either before you take a complaint or before it pays you compensation – which is quite common if it has been systematically mis-selling a product – then you can get compensation from the Financial Services Compensation Scheme. That can take longer still and the compensation cannot be more than £48,000.

Nevertheless, the latest figures from the FSCS shows that in 2004/05 it paid out about £238 million in compensation. Add that to the £246 million cost of the Financial Services Authority and about £40 million for the Ombudsmen Financial and Pensions and you get £524 million. That's the cost of regulating the financial services industry and compensating the public for the mistakes they make and cannot afford to compensate themselves. More than half a billion pounds a year. And it all comes from, guess where, your pocket every time you buy a financial product. Because they are all funded by levies on the industry. It is more than £11 a year for every adult in the UK. So next time you think of the financial services, take a tenner out of your pocket, screw it up into a ball, throw it in the air and try to hit it with a £1 coin. And think, 'thank God for regulation.'

THE END

'How dull it is to pause, to make an end.' (*Ulysses*, Alfred Tennyson, 1842)

But I must stop somewhere. You, however, can carry on. There is a website linked to the book where you can find loads more information and links to things I mention in the book. Some of it is even fun.

CHAPTER ELEVEN

Bits at the Back – And on the Net!

WHAT A DIFFERENCE A-DAY MAKES

You probably do not need to know the rules that applied before A-Day. I just put them in to show you how lucky you are to be thinking of boosting your pension after 6 April 2006. And in case someone you talk to doesn't know the rules have changed. Then you can be smug and say "Weren't those the old rules? Pause. You know, the ones that were scrapped on 6 April 2006?" And it seems such a shame to kill off arcane information without at least a short wake. And of course you may have to fill in or check a tax return for 2005/06 or earlier, so they're not completely otiose.

So for all those very good reasons here is a quick before and after summary:

Before A-day Up to 5 April 2006	After A-Day From 6 April 2006
CONTRIBUTIONS	**CONTRIBUTIONS**
Annual contribution limit **Employer's occupational scheme:** By employer: 100% of earnings* By employee: 15% of earnings* **Stakeholder pension:** By employer and employee combined Your age 35 or less 17.5% of earnings*	**Annual contribution limit** Your annual earnings with a maximum of £215,000. If your earnings are below £3600 or you have no earnings you can still put up to £3600 in. The limit will rise each year reaching £255,000 by 2010/11. No tax relief on any amounts above these limits.

36–45 20% of earnings*
46–50 25% of earnings*
51–55 30% of earnings*
56–60 35% of earnings*
61–74 40% of earnings*
These limits also apply to personal and stakeholder pensions for self-employed people.
You can always put in £3600 however low your earnings, even if you earn nothing.

*Earnings only count up to a cap of £105,600 a year.

Exception: No annual contribution limit in the tax year before you retire but you will only get tax relief on the amount up to your earnings (or £3600 if you earn less than that).

Lifetime limit
Your pension fund value must not exceed £1.5 million. This limit to rise to £1.8 million by 2010/11. Excess taxed at 55%. Salary related schemes calculate the value by multiplying the annual pension by 20, or 25 if already being paid so a pension of £75,000 rising to £90,000 by 2010/11 is allowed.
NB if your pension pot is bigger than this consider if you can protect it.

BENEFITS	BENEFITS
LUMP SUM	**LUMP SUM**
Salary-related occupational schemes up to 3/80ths of final salary for each year of service.	25% of total fund value. The calculation can be complicated for salary related schemes.
Retirement annuity contracts (Pre-1 July 1988, s.226 schemes) Variable percentage of funds, typically 25% but can be more or less.	
Stakeholder and personal pensions 25% of main pension fund 0% of most AVC funds 0% of contracted out benefits	

PENSION	PENSION
No more than 2/3rds of final salary for 30 years' service including value of lump-sum.	**Salary related**: Up to £75,000 rising to £90,000 by 2010/11. **Funded**: whatever can be bought with £1.5 million rising to £1.8 million by 2010/11.
COMMUTATION	COMMUTATION
If your only personal or stakeholder pension fund is less than £2,500 you can take it as a lump sum, with a quarter tax free and the rest taxed as income. If the annual pension from an occupational scheme is less than £260 a year that can also be taken as a lump sum and could all be tax free.	If your total pension funds are worth less than 1% of the lifetime limit (so £15,000, rising to £18,000 in 2010/11), you can take them as a lump sum if you are at least 60 and if you do it all at once. A quarter of the money will be tax – free and the rest taxed as earned income in the year you receive it.

FURTHER HELP AND INFORMATION SOURCES

Think tanks

Pensions Policy Institute

www.pensionspolicyinstitute.org.uk

The one source for factual and statistical information about pensions and the clearest analysis there is of pension problems and solutions.

Pensions Commission

020 7962 8641

www.pensionscommission.org.uk

The official Government pensions think tank – the equivalent of Deep Thought in *The Hitchhiker's Guide to the Galaxy*. Read or download the key reports about the future of pensions and check out its plans.

Ros Altmann
www.rosaltmann.com
An independent policy adviser on pensions, you can read her thoughts and conclusions here. The source for several ideas in this book.

tomorrow's company
www.tomorrowscompany.com
A think tank which has a refreshingly contrarian view. Disputes that there is a looming pensions crisis.

Institute for Fiscal Studies
www.ifs.org.uk
Always factual and unbiased research on many topics including pensions.

ADVICE
Pensions Advisory Service
www.opas.org.uk
0845 601 2913
Paid for by the Government but really excellent. Advice on the phone, news and useful publications.

Age Concern
www.ageconcern.org.uk
Books and information sheets about pensions and other financial matters for people of a certain age. Including some I write.

Help the Aged
www.helptheaged.org.uk
Ditto. Ditto.

GOVERNMENT
Department for Work and Pensions
www.dwp.gov.uk
www.thepensionservice.gov.uk
The Government department responsible for the state pension and most other social security benefits. You can get a state pension

forecast from it and check out the rates of various benefits as well as looking at press releases to see what the Government says it is planning to implement from the Turner Commission report. It also produces useful guides to pensions and benefits, some of which lack detail. The pension service link takes you direct to the pensions pages.

Pension Tracing Service

The Pension Service
Tyneview Park
Whitley Road
Newcastle upon Tyne
NE98 1BA
www.thepensionservice.gov.uk/atoz/atozdetailed/pensiontracing.asp
Now run by the Department for Work and Pensions as part of the Pension Service, hence the long and complicated web address. Holds details of 200,000 pension schemes to help you track down money which might have your name and a very old address on it.

National Statistics

www.statistics.gov.uk
The Government agency which produces figures on wages, employment, inflation (including the Retail Prices Index and the Consumer Prices Index), population and just about everything else about the UK that you can measure or count. Now does a report *Pension Trends*.

The Government Actuary

www.gad.gov.uk
The Government's future cruncher. Life expectancy is his big thing as well as information about National Insurance, the costs of the state pension and public sector pensions.

HM Revenue & Customs

www.hmrc.gov.uk
Devises and enforces lots of the rules relating to pensions. In theory you can find them on its website but navigation can be a real pain. So

far very poor for a simple guide to pensions post A-Day. Also has leaflets on tax and national insurance.

Bank of England
www.bankofengland.co.uk
Sets interest rates and publishes useful statistics on debt – personal lending as it likes to call it.

Houses of Parliament
www.parliament.uk
Every word spoken in Parliament – and in fact a lot that are just written down – is reported in Hansard and you can search this fantastic database free to find phrases, speakers, or topics of debates and written answers to questions. And you can watch proceedings live at www.parliamentlive.tv

REGULATORS
The Financial Services Authority
www.fsa.gov.uk
0845 606 1234
The Government regulator for investments, mortgages and insurance. It sets standards – sometimes very loosely – fines malefactors, and produces loads of useful consumer information and advice not least its comparative tables for major financial products. You can also check up on the credentials of financial advisers and the firms they work for.

The Pensions Regulator
www.thepensionsregulator.gov.uk
Extremely powerful new regulator who can take action against companies which run pension schemes that are under funded, requiring more money to be pumped in and chasing directors or even large shareholders for it. Information here for schemes, members, and the curious.

TRADE BODIES

National Association of Pensions Funds

www.napf.co.uk

The trade body for UK pensions funds and almost all are members. Produces useful data. And is a strong voice in the industry for reform.

Association of British Insurers

www.abi.org.uk

The trade body for the UK insurance industry which means it is something of an apologist for its various iniquities and scandals such as pensions mis-selling and mortgage endowments.

The Actuarial Profession

www.actuaries.org.uk

The umbrella name for the Institute of Actuaries (England and Wales) and the Faculty of Actuaries in Scotland. Useful but often rather obscure reports on pensions and life expectancy. But if you want to become an actuary, a good starting place for information!

FINANCIAL ADVISERS

IFA Promotion Ltd (IFAP)

www.unbiased.co.uk

0800 085 3250

Phone their hotline for a list of independent financial advisers in your home or work area or log on and specify what kind of adviser you want.

Personal Finance Society

www.thepfs.org

A trade body for independent financial advisers. Develops qualifications and sets exams. Can also help find an adviser and has useful advice and information.

Financial Services Skills Council
www.fssc.org.uk
020 7216 7366
Everything to do with improving the qualifications and skills of people in the financial services industry.

Annuity Direct
www.annuitydirect.co.uk
0500 50 65 75
A commercial site of an Independent Financial Adviser. Easy-to-use quotes for pension annuities to help you find the best.

COMPARISON SITES
Moneyfacts
www.moneyfacts.co.uk
The least financially motivated of the comparison sites – apart from the Financial Services Authority of course. Brilliant for cash investments, mortgages, credit cards, and loans.

Moneysupermarket
www.moneysupermarket.com
This site makes its money from visitors clicking through to look at or buy products.

Moneysavingexpert.com
www.moneysavingexpert.com
This eccentric site is not so much for anoraks as for those that sleep in them too. Join the debate on how to save money on everything. Unique information on finding the best deals in credit cards, loans and mortgages.

The Motley Fool
www.fool.co.uk
Some of the best unbiased information and discussion about investments and personal finance. Also makes its living from click throughs and comparisons.

DEBT PROBLEMS
Consumer Credit Counselling Service
www.cccs.co.uk
0800 138 1111
Never ever ever pay anyone to help you sort out your debts. Visit this site. They don't judge you and really can help.

National Debtline
www.nationaldebtline.co.uk
0808 808 4000
Ditto.

INVESTMENT
Investment Management Association
www.investmentfunds.org.uk
020 8207 1361
For factsheets and guides to saving and investing in unit trusts and OEICs.

Association of Investment Trust Companies (AITC)
www.aitc.co.uk
0800 085 8520
For a range of factsheets explaining various aspects of investment trusts.

Ethical Investment Research Service
www.eiris.org
020 7840 5700
Publishes a range of publications, including a guide to choosing a financial adviser.

Social Investment Forum
www.uksif.org
Also promotes socially responsible investing.

Association of Residential Letting Agents
www.arla.co.uk

01494 431680

Invented the whole concept of Buy-to-Let, produces useful help and guidance on what it involves and an index of returns you can expect – much of which is very difficult to understand.

FTSE International
www.ftse.com

More information than any mortal could want about stock market indices. But don't expect to find the figures themselves. Those can be found at http://uk.finance.yahoo.com.

WHEN THINGS GO WRONG
Pension Protection Fund
www.pensionprotectionfund.org.uk

All salary-related pension schemes have to join and pay a hefty annual fee to the PPF which pays out when a company goes bust and a pension fund is wound up. An often frustrating website which should, but doesn't always, contain the information you need about what it's doing and who can get what.

Financial Ombudsman Service (FOS)
South Quay Plaza

183 Marsh Wall

London E14 9SR

0845 080 1800

www.financial-ombudsman.org.uk

Provides consumers with a free independent service for resolving disputes with financial firms.

The Pensions Ombudsman
www.pensions-ombudsman.org.uk

020 7834 9144

Deals with complaints about how a pension scheme is run.

Financial Services Compensation Scheme (FSCS)
www.fscs.org.uk
020 7892 7300
Pays compensation to customers of a financial services company which goes out of business.

THE MEDIA
Money Box
www.bbc.co.uk/moneybox
Weekly financial programme on Radio 4. Brilliant. What more can I say? Oh. I present it. Here you can listen to the current programme and read transcripts of past programmes. Also check out Working Lunch BBC 2 weekday lunchtimes.

Newspapers
Many people rely on journalists for financial information and even advice. Which, given that we are one of the least trusted professions down there with politicians and estate agents, says a lot about how much people trust real financial advisers. But you should read the personal finance supplements usually found with the Saturday and Wednesday editions and of course with the Sundays. If I had to choose, which I don't, I would recommend Money in *The Guardian* on Saturday and Money Mail in Wednesday's *Daily Mail*.

Google
www.google.co.uk
For anything else, use Google. The UK address lets you just search UK based pages.

INDEX